ALSO BY EDITH GROSSMAN
The Antipoetry of Nicanor Parra
Why Translation Matters

SELECTED TRANSLATIONS BY EDITH GROSSMAN
Love in the Time of Cholera (Gabriel García Márquez)
Memories of My Melancholy Whores (Gabriel García Márquez)
The Feast of the Goat (Mario Vargas Llosa)
The Dream of the Celt (Mario Vargas Llosa)
Destiny and Desire (Carlos Fuentes)
Happy Families (Carlos Fuentes)
Dancing to "Almendra" (Mayra Montero)
The Red of His Shadow (Mayra Montero)
A Manuscript of Ashes (Antonio Muñoz Molina)
In the Night of Time (Antonio Muñoz Molina)
Loves that Bind (Julián Ríos)
Monstruary (Julián Ríos)
Red April (Santiago Roncagliolo)
Hi, This Is Conchita (Santiago Roncagliolo)
Nada (Carmen Laforet)
Complete Works and Other Stories (Augusto Monterroso)
The Ingenious Gentleman and Poet Federico García Lorca Ascends to Hell
(Carlos Rojas)
The Adventures and Misadventures of Maqroll (Álvaro Mutis)
Caracol Beach (Eliseo Alberto)
Don Quixote (Miguel de Cervantes)
The Solitudes (Luis de Góngora)
The Golden Age: Poems of the Spanish Renaissance (Various)

Praise for
Edith Grossman's Translation of the Works of Sor Juana

"Edith Grossman is a marvel. With the greatest artistry she has given vibrant, contemporary voice to Sor Juana, legendary proto-feminist bard of seventeenth-century Mexico, capturing the wit, tenderness, and religious fervor of her work."
—Susan Bernofsky, translator of Kafka's *The Metamorphosis*

"Edith Grossman's judicious selection and eloquent translation of the writings of Sor Juana Inés de la Cruz will bring many new readers to the work of this 'Tenth Muse,' the first major poet of the New World. The poems chosen for inclusion illustrate her extraordinary range, and the epistolary exchange between 'Sor Filotea' and Sor Juana reveals the perilous context of her writing life."
—Charles Martin, translator of Ovid's *Metamorphoses* and cotranslator of *The Bhagavad Gita*

"A welcome new translation of the charismatic Sor Juana Inés de la Cruz! Historians of feminism will be especially drawn to this version of her classic, impassioned letter to the misogynistic bishop whom she mistakenly thought was 'Sor Filotea.' "
—Sandra M. Gilbert, coeditor of *The Norton Anthology of Literature by Women*

"Grossman's translation is extraordinarily fluent and accessible, rendering Sor Juana's seventeenth-century prose accurately and felicitously, and in an idiom that avoids fussy archaisms."
—Wayne Rebhorn, translator of *The Decameron*

"Edith Grossman's translation has given the writings an accessible but also exquisite and mysterious presence for English-language readers. Her translation retains the grace of great thought, embedded in glorious language, and embellished with delectable playfulness. Sor Juana wrote with the relaxed elegance that is the real soul of eloquence. Nothing of that is lost in this translation. We have in this *Selected Works* a lovely, delightful, and profound book of world literature, very much 'of use' here and now."

—Lyn Hejinian, author of *A Border Comedy* and *The Language of Inquiry*

"Edith Grossman's new translation of the seventeenth-century Mexican nun/poet/scholar known today as the Tenth Muse and First Feminist of Latin America offers the English-speaking audience an accessible Sor Juana. Grossman's mastery as a translator decodes the baroque Castilian of the original and conveys Sor Juana's lyricism, rhetoric, and logic, as well as 'the enigmatic core of her life and work,' in crisp contemporary English."

—Alicia Gaspar de Alba, author of *Sor Juana's Second Dream*

Sor Juana Inés de la Cruz

SELECTED WORKS

TRANSLATED BY *Edith Grossman*

INTRODUCTION BY *Julia Alvarez*

W. W. NORTON & COMPANY

Independent Publishers Since 1923

New York · London

For information about permission to reproduce selections from this book,
write to Permissions, W. W. Norton & Company, Inc.,
500 Fifth Avenue, New York, NY 10110

For information about special discounts for bulk purchases,
please contact W. W. Norton Special Sales at
specialsales@wwnorton.com or 800-233-4830

Manufacturing by LSC Harrisonburg
Book design by Marysarah Quinn
Production manager: Julia Druskin

Library of Congress Cataloging-in-Publication Data

Juana Inés de la Cruz, Sister, 1651–1695.
[Poetry. Selections]
Sor Juana Inés de la Cruz : selected works / translated by Edith
Grossman ; introduction by Julia Alvarez. — First edition.
pages cm
ISBN 978-0-393-24175-4 (hardcover)
I. Grossman, Edith, 1936– translator. II. Title.
PQ7296.J6A6 2014
861'.3—dc23

2014025634

ISBN 978-0-393-35188-0 pbk.

W. W. Norton & Company, Inc.
500 Fifth Avenue, New York, N.Y. 10110
www.wwnorton.com

W. W. Norton & Company Ltd.
15 Carlisle Street, London W1D 3BS

6 7 8 9 0

CONTENTS

INTRODUCTION

Response to Sor Juana Inés de la Cruz
After Reading Her Poems

If I could pay you, señora, something of what I owe you, I believe I would pay you in full by telling you this. . . .

Most Eminent Sor Juana,

You say everything so much better yourself, as I now know, not just from reading *about* you but finally reading your own words, that it is daunting to address a letter to you. As you can see, I even begin it by quoting you! Like you—and begging your pardon for this and all ensuing comparisons of my puny flicker of a light to your blazing sun—I was tempted by a sense of my unworthiness to keep silent. But I have been compelled to break that silence in payment of my debt of gratitude to you. As you will note from what follows, I speak of you indirectly in the third person, aware of the respect I owe you, and also, as you remind us in many of your writings, of the fate of the foolhardy who fly too close to the sun. Only in the opening and closing of this confession, do I dare cross that boundary of modesty and cleave you to myself, for surely, as a passionate reader, you know that we take the best works into the intimacy of our souls and make them our own. Here then is my confession to you on the occasion of finally reading this generous and accessible selection of your work:

When I was a girl, and I would speak out of turn, especially in my own defense or in defense of some supposedly indefensible person or idea, my mother would caution me, *"No te pongas tú de Sor Juana!"* Don't you try to be a Sor Juana! I had no idea who Sor Juana was, and when questioned, my mother, who was not a reader, had little to say about Sor Juana's writings. But Mami knew the outlines of this famous nun's story. A female who also couldn't hold her tongue and came to a bad end.

Sor Juana entered that very small pantheon of personal saints I didn't yet know I was accumulating, seedbed for what was to come (Joan of Arc; Scheherazade of the *Arabian Nights*; the intrepid, star-chasing *princesita* Margarita of Rubén Darío's poem). But unlike these others, who were in my prayer book or in storybooks or in poems I was taught to recite, Sor Juana was nowhere except my mother's admonitions. I assumed she, too, had been burned at a stake, or beheaded, because that was the only bad end I could imagine when I was told that she had been "silenced."

I was not yet a reader, still living in Spanish, years and another country and language away from becoming a writer, so I had not yet discovered that being silenced is a kind of death. Interestingly, my initial encounter with this first great poet of the Americas and brilliant intellect of Spanish letters, known by her own contemporaries as the Tenth Muse, was as a kind of bogeywoman, marched out to teach me the risks of having a mind of my own. Sor Juana's example was usually accompanied by the popular *refrán* (saying) *"El clavo que sobresale siempre recibe un martillazo."* The nail that sticks out always gets hit by a hammer.

We were living in a dictatorship, where being outspoken could bring you, male or female, certain imprisonment and a likely tortured death, so my mother had every reason to fear a child who liked to tell stories and argue against authority.

Years later, having escaped the dictatorship, already at home in the United States and in what had become my dominant language, English, I learned more about this iconic figure. Sor Juana was one of a number of gifted women who had suffered hardship and censorship for their talents. In those heady days of my apprenticeship as a young poet in the early 1970s, emboldened by the feminist movement, I claimed her as one of my influences. But again it was her biography, not her writings, which dominated my imagination. And, of course, she held a special place in my iconography of models, because among my many literary godmothers (Emily Dickinson, Jane Austen, George Eliot, Virginia Woolf, among others), Sor Juana was the only one who came from my part of the world.

Empty of substance as my claim was—I had yet to read a word she had written—I was fiercely proud of her. Unlike the imagined Judith Shakespeare of Virginia Woolf's *A Room of One's Own*, who never went to London or wrote her plays and sonnets, Sor Juana managed to get herself to Mexico City, be invited into the viceroyal court, pursue her studies, and write works celebrated throughout the Spanish-speaking empire, a big part of the world back then. She was definitely not one of the "many Theresas" George Eliot describes in her prelude to *Middlemarch*, who because of "meanness of opportunity . . . sank unwept into oblivion. . . . A cygnet reared uneasily among the ducklings . . . [who] never [found] the living stream in fellowship." Hers was the astonishing case of a poor, illegitimate, colonial female, to boot, who turned around the meanness of her situation and became the literary star of her time. But then, oh boy, was Mami ever right (again!). Sor Juana had come to a bad end: eventually falling out of favor, unprotected, pressured to sell her books, stop writing, confess, and renounce her sinful life (signing her self-condemnation with her own blood). Two years later, she was dead at forty-six, after ministering to her fellow sisters in the convent stricken by the plague. So this is what happened to women who followed a calling and attained a voice! Sor Juana's story both thrilled me and terrified me.

But this telenovela of her life was really all I knew of Sor Juana, a case of putting the biographical cart before the Pegasus of her poetry. Like the life story of another of my muses, Emily Dickinson (one whose poems I had read), Sor Juana's biography can be so intriguing that her work can become eclipsed by it. Interestingly, Sor Juana's fate went in an opposite trajectory from Emily Dickinson's, who became famous and known after her death, one of the luminaries of the English-speaking literary canon. Sor Juana, on the other hand, enjoyed wide acclaim during her lifetime in the second half of the seventeenth century in the viceroyalty of New Spain, as well as in Spain, where her work was first published. But then for nearly two hundred years after her death, she and her works were forgotten, until the Spanish-speaking world began to rediscover her in the early twentieth century.

But among monolingual English readers her work was little known. In the early 1980s, inspired by the growing feminist movement, a few translations appeared in anthologies of women's writing. Octavio Paz's masterly biography, *Sor Juana or, The Traps of Faith*, published in 1982 in Spanish and in English translation in 1988, did much to champion this "universal writer" and complicate and contextualize the work and the life. Then came the movie in 1990, *Yo, La Peor de Todas* ("I, the worst of them all," the phrase that Sor Juana used to describe herself in her profession of self-condemnation)—still a case of the biography eclipsing the work. In my ignorance, I, too, was contributing to the forgotten fate of her writings.

But I was caught in the dilemma of many first-generation immigrants who remain identified with their origin culture, but are not fluent in their native language. Culturally Latina, I had become English dominant, which in the sometimes charged identity politics of the 1980s and '90s, felt like a betrayal of what should have been my mother tongue. Like Sor Juana, I and many Latina writers had a number of conflicting identities to negotiate: our Hispanic roots (*Hispanic* itself became a contested term) with our independent, Americanized lifestyles; our feminism with our feeling of loyalty toward a cultural inheritance with problematic patriarchal and *machista* aspects; our English language, which implied assimilation, and brought us a mainstream readership with our Spanglish insertions and Latino characters and content, which set us apart and bound us to our often regional *comunidades*. And unlike many of my fellow Latinas, who had been here in the USA "forever," I had been raised in the Dominican Republic for the first ten years, so I had no excuse for not continuing to study my childhood Spanish. It was my secret I was too embarrassed to reveal: I wanted to claim Sor Juana as one of my influences, but since I do not read easily in Spanish, and especially the Spanish of the seventeenth-century Baroque period, I was hostage to whatever samplings of her work made their way into English translation.

But just as Sor Juana found her vicereines to gift her with books and intellectual resources and fellowship, I, too, found mine. Much of my knowledge of Spanish-language writers has come via English translations, and none more than those of Edith Grossman, who has given me, as well as countless others, access to those texts. Works as varied as Miguel de Cervantes's *Don Quixote*; Gabriel García Márquez's *Love in the Time of Cholera* and *News of a Kidnapping*; Mario Vargas Llosa's *The Feast of the Goat* (about the very dictatorship I grew up in); and the novels of a favorite contemporary Cuban writer, Mayra Montero. What I've always admired about Edith Grossman's translations is their ease and elegance, their clarity and accessibility: one has the sense of hearing the original without the interference of a costumed style trying too hard to re-create the voice and instead betraying the effort of the impersonation.

Toward the end of his life, Stanley Kunitz remarked that he wanted "to write poems that are natural, luminous, deep, spare. I dream of an art so transparent that you can look through it and see the world." Hard enough to achieve in one's own language, and near impossible in translation. This is Edith Grossman's art: we feel we are in touch with the original text. It might be why, a story that may be apocryphal, García Márquez supposedly claimed that he preferred reading his own novels in her (as well as Gregory Rabassa's) English translations.

And so now at last I hold your work in my hands, Sor Juana. I can hear your voice, the sassiness of the epigrams, the archness and humor and intimacy of the décimas and redondillas and ballads; the elegant turns of the sonnets; and everywhere a mind at play, its sparkling intelligence, its passionate longings, its wide-ranging curiosity, even its haunting silences. As your countryman and biographer Paz once observed, "an unread author is an author who is the victim of the worst kind of censorship." I am no longer contributing to that censorship! I can, therefore, address you here in closing with a homely familiarity that is not a lack of respect but a mark of the intimacy I now feel with the work itself.

But I am also grateful for the inspiration of your biography, the example of a woman who dared and proved her excellence, whose voice comes down the centuries and speaks to us today. We are reminded daily that the struggle for female education is ongoing. The world is still full of

Malalas facing violence for wanting to go to school. It is in order to read works like yours that they feel compelled to follow your example. For this is your truest, most treasured legacy, the work itself. In keeping with another of your epithets, the "Mexican Phoenix," here you are, reborn again, this time in English in these translations.

—Julia Alvarez
September 30, 2013

TRANSLATOR'S NOTE

I.

Why bring out another translation of works by Sor Juana Inés de la Cruz (1651–1695)? Perhaps the most legitimate and straightforward answer to the question is this: Why not?

Works of literary art don't appear to age—generations of readers pore over them, embrace them, and make them part of their lives—but, paradoxically, translations of those same works can become time-worn. Some commentators claim that the maximum shelf life of a translation is thirty years. I won't argue for or against the number—it's not an issue I've looked into with any care—but the fact that translations do age seems indisputable. Just consider the surprising number of versions in English of great works of literature by Homer, Dante, Cervantes, Goethe, Baudelaire, Chekhov, or Neruda. What, other than the sense that a new translation is needed for contemporary readers, could possibly send translators and their publishers back, over and over again, to the same literary wells?

Agreeing to undertake any literary translation can often seem the height of temerity, an act of hubris doomed to calamitous failure. After all, for years translators have been admonished with devastating frequency that the endeavor is impossible, that we have embarked on a fool's errand, that our work invariably betrays the original. Even so, we persevere. This new translation exemplifies the tenacity of our resolve.

Sor Juana is a profoundly enigmatic author whose position as an indispensable writer has not been challenged in our time, and whose compositions have already been brought over into English by some of our most accomplished translators. And this leads us to pose the question again: Why a new edition of her work? Which brings up a related question that loomed very large as I worked on this book: Does the translation of her work present particular, *sui generis* problems?

Called the Tenth Muse by her contemporaries—a name that still resonates—Sor Juana continues to perplex us. Unlike Luis de Góngora and Francisco de Quevedo, two of the great poets of the Spanish Baroque who inspired her, she was largely self-taught. Far from being a provincial autodidact, however, she had a prodigious intellect, a vast store of scriptural, theological, classical, and contemporary knowledge, immense skill as a writer in a broad range of genres, and a real penchant for study and scholarship, with a special proclivity for the sciences and music. She was a nun, but not a cloistered one, and regularly held an elite salon in the convent's locutory. Further, she acquired thousands of volumes for what apparently was the largest private library in the viceroyalty of New Spain (later Mexico). Yet in spite of all her acumen, learning, and astute intelligence, she somehow failed to take into account the depth of sexist bigotry that prevailed in every sector of society, including the Church to which she had devoted her life. Why did she allow herself to be caught in the snares set by a misogynistic hierarchy, embodied in the person of Manuel Fernández de Santa Cruz, Bishop of Puebla, who once had been her friend and associate but who attacked her in a portentous letter, purportedly by another nun, the fictional Sor Filotea, after he had asked her to write a theological challenge to a male cleric and then published it without her permission? Her proto-feminist *Response to Sor Filotea*, an impassioned and erudite defense of a woman's right to study, develop her mind, and commit her thoughts to paper, did nothing to dissuade the Church authorities from punishing what they saw as intolerable arrogance and undue independence of thought. She was obliged to disperse her library, stop writing, and submit to the discipline of harsh physical and spiritual chastisement. She had crossed a line into forbidden territory and could not be permitted to emerge from that trespass unscathed.

In his groundbreaking book on Sor Juana, Octavio Paz offers an intriguing interpretation of the impact of this all-encompassing repression on her writing:

> . . . in addition to the anonymous community of ordinary readers, there is a group of privileged readers called the Archbishop, the Inquisitor . . . they had as much influence on Sor Juana Inés de la Cruz as her admirers. . . . Her dread readers are a part— and a significant part—of her work. Her work tells us something, but to understand that something we must realize that it is utterance surrounded by silence: the silence of the *things that cannot be said*. The things she cannot say are determined by the invisible presence of her dread readers. When we read Sor Juana, we

must recognize the silence surrounding her words. That silence is not absence of meaning; on the contrary, what cannot be said is anything that touches not only on the orthodoxy of the Catholic Church but also on the ideas, interests, and passions of its princes and its Orders. Sor Juana's words are written in the presence of a prohibition; that prohibition is embodied in an orthodoxy supported by a bureaucracy of prelates and judges. An understanding of Sor Juana's work must include an understanding of the prohibitions her work confronts. Her speech leads us to what cannot be said. . . .[1]

The baffling challenge to the translator of her writing is how to reproduce "the silence of the *things that cannot be said*" in another language. This isn't a Zen conundrum, not the sound of silence or of one hand clapping. On the contrary, this is the terrified silence created by fear of the Holy Office, the constant, intimidating presence of the Inquisition. What precisely, we must ask, did Sor Juana *not* say in order to conform to the strictures of an oppressive society and of what she always referred to as her "status" or her "state"—that is, her position as a member of a religious order? The question must be asked, but the answer is not easy to find. The issue of that silence may well be one of the factors that continue to draw both translators and readers to her writing; the ongoing

1 Octavio Paz, *Sor Juana or, The Traps of Faith*, tr. Margaret Sayers Peden (Cambridge, Mass.: Harvard University Press, 1988), pp. 5–6.

effort to decipher words not spoken penetrates to the enigmatic core of her life and work.

2.

I'd like to mention very briefly some of the choices I made as I developed the voice of this translation. My usual practice in translating poetry is to focus on rhythm and meter and give much shorter shrift to rhyme, not because it lacks importance (rhyme is actually an integral part of a poem's rhythmic structure) but because for me it is extremely difficult to re-create in English the abundant rhymes, both assonant and consonant, that proliferate in Spanish and seem to be there for the taking. Not so in English. A poetic genius like Yeats makes rhyming seem a simple, natural matter, no more difficult than drawing breath, but for lesser mortals, moving from an easily rhymed language to one in which finding rhymes can best be described as arduous is an excruciating process. Even more discouraging is the sad fact that, more often than not, a translation that stresses the re-creation of rhyme begins to resemble not the source poem but doggerel plagiarized from a cheap greeting card. Then too, lines can become drastically convoluted in a translator's desperate effort to create rhymes that convey the sense of the original. Consequently, as I have written elsewhere, experience has led me to concentrate on the rhythm of the poem and take as my own the wisdom found in the Duke Ellington tune: "It don't mean a thing if it ain't got that swing."

Rhythm in a poem is, in part, a function of the meter in which the piece is written. Spanish meter is determined by the number of syllables in a line; English meter, on the other hand, is based on the number of feet—that is, the clustering of a stressed syllable and its attendant unstressed syllables. English versification is different from the meters found in Romance languages, but even though they are dissimilar, it has always seemed important to me to try to re-create the syllable count of Spanish meter in the English-language version of a poem and, if possible, to place the stresses in the English line where they are found in the Spanish. Over the years, this has become a guiding principle when I translate metric poetry. The poems in this volume are no exception. Blank verse raises other issues, but they are irrelevant here since all of Sor Juana's poetry uses both rhyme and traditional meter.

Turning to the translation of Golden Age prose, in general I find it important to avoid a fustian imitation of Elizabethan language and to use contemporary English instead. Sor Juana wrote what was, for her, up-to-date, not archaic Spanish. I don't believe a translation acquires authenticity, accuracy, or artfulness if it is written in an invented seventeenth-century idiom that is cumbersome for the translator to create, onerous for the reader to peruse, and not at all like the language used by the original author. Further, what Sor Juana has to say in her prose is so crucially important that I wanted nothing to interfere with your apprehension of it, and I certainly did not want to place any obstacles in the way of your being moved by it.

My sincere wish is that your mind is nourished and your heart filled by what you read in this new translation of selected works by the Tenth Muse of Mexico.

3.

Finally, I would like to express my gratitude to the eminent scholars whose immense erudition made possible the editions of Sor Juana's work that I used for this translation. These outstanding works are:

Sor Juana Inés de la Cruz. *Obras completas*. Prol. Francisco Monterde, México, DF: Editorial Porrúa, 2004 (based on the text established in the 1951–1957 edition by the Fondo de Cultura Económica, edited by Alfonso Méndez Plancarte).

Sor Juana Inés de la Cruz. *Poesía, teatro, pensamiento*. Edited and with an introduction by Georgina Sabat de Rivers and Elias Rivers. Madrid: Fundación Biblioteca de Literatura Universal, Espasa Calpe, 2004.

The Answer / La Repuesta (Expanded Edition). Edited and translated by Electa Arenal and Amanda Powell. New York: Feminist Press at CUNY, 2009.

A Sor Juana Anthology. Translated by Alan S. Trueblood. Cambridge, Mass.: Harvard University Press, 1990.

Sor Juana Inés de la Cruz: *Selected Writings*. Edited by Pamela Kirk Rappaport. Mahwah, N.J.: Paulist Press, 2005.

The poems in this volume are numbered according to the system used in the Porrúa edition; Georgina de Sabat Rivers and Elias Rivers provide us with texts that have invaluable notes and commentary.

I would also like to thank Anna More for her invaluable help, as well as my editor, Carol Bemis, and her assistant, Thea Goodrich, who demonstrated admirable patience and a meticulous attention to detail. Knowing that these three were behind me was very reassuring on what often seemed a rocky and perilous path.

—Edith Grossman
New York City

BALLADS

(Ballads, called *romances* in Spanish,
are composed of an indefinite number of
stanzas of generally octosyllabic lines,
the odd lines unrhymed, the even lines
using assonant rhyme.)

BALLAD 1

Prologue to the reader from the author, who composed and sent it with the same haste used for those already copied, obeying the supreme command of her extraordinary patron, Her Excellency the Countess of Paredes,[1] that they be made public: this Sor Juana had denied her verses which, like the poet herself, were in the safekeeping of the countess, for the poet barely had a single draft in her possession

These verses, my dearest reader,
dedicated to your delight,
have but one virtue in them:
I know how imperfect they are,

I do not wish to discuss them
or even commend them to you,
for that would mean wishing to pay
them attention unmerited.

I do not seek your gratitude
for, if truth be told, you should not
esteem something I never deemed
worthy of being in your hands.

1 María Luisa, Countess of Paredes, was the wife of Tomás de la Cerda, third Marquis de la Laguna, who was the Viceroy of Mexico from 1680 to 1686.

I grant and cede you liberty
if you should wish to censure them;
after all, to conclude, you are
free, and I have concluded too.

Nothing enjoys greater freedom
than the human understanding;
if God does not violate mind
then why would I even try?

Say all that you wish about them,
for the more merciless you are
in finding fault, the greater your
obligation will be to me,

for then you will owe to my Muse
that most flavorsome of dishes
—speaking ill of another—as
an old adage of the court says.

I am always at your service,
whether I please you or do not:
if I please you, you are amused;
if not, you can speak ill of me.

I could easily say to you
as an excuse, that I did not

have the time to revise them,
they were copied so rapidly;

they are written by diverse hands,
and some, being the hands of boys,
kill the sense in such a way that
the word is no more than a corpse;

when I have written them myself,
it has been in the brief space
of leisure that can be bought from
the exigencies of my state;

for my health is poor and I am
so often interrupted that
even as I say this my pen
races along at breakneck speed.

But none of this is to the point,
for you will think I am boasting
that perhaps they might have been good
if I had composed them slowly;

I do not wish you to think that,
no, but only that I brought them
to light in order to comply,
to obey another's command.

True, believe it or not, this is
not a question of life or death
to me, and to conclude, you will
do whatever occurs to you.

And farewell, for this merely shows
you a small sample of the cloth:
but if the piece does not please you,
then do not unroll the whole bolt.

BALLAD 2

She acknowledges the excesses of a good deal of erudition, which she fears is useless even to learning and injurious to living

Let us pretend I am happy,
melancholy Thought, for a while;
perhaps you can persuade me, though
I know the contrary is true:

for since on mere apprehension
they say all suffering depends,
if you imagine good fortune
you will not be so downcast.

Let my understanding at times
allow me to rest a while,
and let my wits not always be
opposed to my own advantage.

All people have opinions and
judgments so multitudinous,
that when one states this is black,
the other proves it is white.

Some find attractive precisely
what others deem an annoyance;

an alleviation for one
is bothersome for another.

One who is sad criticizes
the happy man as frivolous;
and one who is happy derides
the sad man and his suffering.

The two philosophers of Greece[2]
offered perfect proofs of this truth:
for what caused laughter in one man
occasioned tears in the other.

The contradiction has been famed
for centuries beyond number,
yet which of the two was correct
has so far not been determined;

instead, into their two factions
all people have been recruited,
temperament dictating which
band each person will adhere to.

---

2 Heraclitus of Ephesus (c. 540–c. 480 BCE) and Democritus of Abdera
(c. 460–370 BCE), pre-Socratic philosophers who claimed that life was a cause,
respectively, for weeping or for laughter.

One says that the inconstant world
is worthy only of laughter;
another, that its misfortunes
are only to be lamented.

A proof is found for everything,
a reason on which to base it;
and nothing has a good reason
since there is reason for so much.

All people are equal judges;
being both equal and varied,
there is no one who can decide
which argument is true and right.

Since no one can adjudicate,
why do you think, mistakenly,
that God entrusted you alone
with the decision in this case?

Oh why, inhuman and severe,
and acting against yourself, in
the choice between bitter and sweet
do you wish to choose the bitter?

If my understanding is my
own, why must I always find it
so slow and dull about relief,
so sharp and keen about distress?

Discursive reason is a sword
quite effective at both ends:
with the point of the blade it kills;
the pommel on the hilt protects.

If you, aware of the danger,
wish to wield the point of the sword,
how can the steel blade be to blame
for the evil acts of your hand?

Knowing how to create subtle,
specious reasons is not knowledge;
true knowledge consists only in
choosing salutary virtue.

Scrutinizing all misfortunes
and examining bad omens
achieves nothing but the growth of
the bad through anticipation.

In future deliberations
our attention, grown more subtle,

will imagine threatened attacks
as more alarming than the risks.

How blithesome is the ignorance
of one who, unlearned but wise,
deems his affliction, his nescience
all he does not know, as sacred!

The most daring flights of genius
do not always soar assured when
they seek a throne in the fire
and find a grave in copious tears.

For knowledge is also a vice:
if it is not constantly curbed,
and if this is not acknowledged,
the greater the havoc it wreaks;

and if the flight is not brought down,
fed and fattened on subtleties
it will forget the essential
for the sake of the rare and strange.

If a skilled hand does not prevent
the growth of a thickly leafed tree,
its proliferating branches
will steal the substance of the fruit.

If the bulk of ballast does not
impede the speed of a swift ship,
that flight creates the headlong fall
from a most precipitous height.

It is futile amenity:
what does the flowering field care
if Autumn finds no fruit as long
as May can display its blossoms?

What benefit to intellect
to gestate so many offspring,
if that multitude is followed
by ill-fated miscarriages?

And perforce this great misfortune
must be followed by mischance:
the one who gestates will be left
if not dead, then gravely injured.

Our intellect is like fire:
deeply ungrateful to matter,
flame consumes more matter the
brighter the fire appears.

So rebellious a vassal to
its own legitimate Lord,

that fire transforms the weapons of
its defense into offenses.

This appalling, daunting practice,
this harsh and onerous toil
God gave to the children of men
for the sake of their discipline.

What mad ambition carries us,
having forgotten who we are?
If we live for so short a time,
why do we wish to know so much?

Oh, if there were only a school
or seminary where they taught
classes in how not to know
as they teach classes in knowing.

How happily the man would live
who with languid circumspection
would simply laugh at the menace
of the influence of the stars!

Let us learn about not knowing,
O Thought, for we then discover
that for all I add to discourse
I usurp as much from my years.

The Vicereine having already baptized her child, the poet offers
congratulations on his birth

I have not wanted, dear Lysi,[3]
to send my felicitations
for the child God has given you
until you returned him to God:[4]

in your religion, señora,
though your beauty engenders him,
you would not want to call him yours
if he does not belong to God.

It speaks well of your piety
that you wish to call your son,
His Excellency, *child of the*
Church, although born legitimate;[5]

and having been born in the light,
until there dawns above him
the light of Grace, you do not prize
unduly the light of Nature.

---

3 Lysi, or Lisi, is a standard name used in pastural poetry of the Golden Age.
4 That is, until the child was baptized and therefore "returned" to God.
5 Offspring born out of wedlock were called "children of the Church."

In grace you enjoy him, aeons
of such great Christian purity
that Grace received increases
and Grace acquired is not lost.

You see, in his behavior, the
piety and greatness, as did
Olympias in Alexander,
and Helena in Constantine.

Entwine in heroic mingling
of arms and letters, the laurels
of warlike Mars with the olives
of the learned Minerva.

May he be the glory of his
land, the envy of all others;
and America, with his gifts,
will vanquish those of all others.

May he bring his high lineage
in a propitious moment to
the Occident; Europe closely
mingles so many royal bloodlines.

Let a proud America raise
high the head that wears a crown,

and let the Mexican Eagle
spread its great imperial wings,

for now in its royal palace
where all the grandeur of pagan
Moctezumas lies, Catholic
Cerda[6] scions are being born.

Let this generous Cupid blossom,
and grow in valor and beauty;
he is born of Mars and Venus,
may he favor Mars and Venus.

May Bellona give him weapons,
and Eros offer his arrows,
Alcides turn over his club,
Apollo offer his knowledge.

Let this new Alexander grow,
this pious Aeneas live long,
this greater Pompilius endure,
this heroic Maecenas excel.

---

6 The viceroy of New Spain from 1680 to 1686, and the father of the child cele-
brated in this poem, was Tomás de la Cerda, third Marquis de la Laguna.

His birth in the month of July
was not by chance: necessity
ruled that, being so great a Prince,
he be born a Julius Caesar.[7]

Now I imagine I see him
in the years of early childhood,
learning to read in the primer
until he resembles Cato,[8]

and since that age was deemed by the
Romans as full grown and mature,
they traded medals and pretext
for the toga of true manhood.[9]

Here his valor and eloquence
will surely be seen in him,
the Campaigns that will astonish,
the Schools in which he will excel;

here the world will surely see in
his right hand a confusion of

---

7 The wordplay in Spanish is based on *Julio* being the word for both July and Julius.
8 Another example of wordplay: a reading primer is a *catón*, which is also the
Spanish word for Cato.
9 Medals were worn by children in Rome to protect them from spells; the *praetexta*
was the garb of boys, while the toga was worn by men.

the flourishes of a pen and
the violent strokes of a sword;

here the contrary professions
will surely call and summon him,
Peace on account of his prudence,
War on account of his valor;

here the better Julius in
erudition and prudence will
surely be his own chronicler
and write of his deeds and prowess;[10]

here there will surely be seen
a new, unheard-of miracle:
the addition of more to more
is what the Mexican grows on.

Here if I live long enough,
even if I walk with crutches,
my Muse surely intends to add
quill pens and language to his Fame.

---

10 The reference here is to Julius Caesar's *Gallic Wars*, in which the author was also the protagonist.

And here I cease writing to you,
and let this long argument end
with the Boy living eternities
and you being there to see it.

To the same most excellent lady (the Countess of Galve), sending her
an embroidered shoe, in the Mexican style, and a gift of chocolate

> Throwing down a glove, señora,
> is a signal of defiance;
> so that throwing down a shoe
> must be a sign of submission.
>
> The wish to take another's hand
> indicates a certain boldness;
> but humbling oneself at her feet
> demonstrates one's submission.
>
> Yet it is true that in your feet
> this principle is proven false,
> for they increase in their substance
> and decrease in the sound they make.
>
> Rising to the soles of your feet
> is so haughty an intention,
> that on high one does not possess
> knowledge of the danger involved.
>
> Not the one who recklessly dared
> to circle round the whirling blue,

nor one who tried to defy the
burning orb with feathers and wax,[11]

could give the warning learned from their
experience of the downfall;
for a lesser plunge cannot serve
as a precautionary tale.

But I fly too high, and to where?
It seems now that I follow them,
for the path, twisting and turning,
takes me so far from my intent.

I mean, señora, that the day
of that most holy of Bishops[12]
when miracles were no such thing
because they arose constantly,

is celebrated with liquor
and this gift, while not very blessed,

11 The first reference is to Phaethon, son of Helios, god of the sun, who attempted
to drive the sun's chariot across the sky and came so close to Earth that the planet
almost caught fire. Zeus killed him with a thunderbolt. The second is to Icarus,
son of Daedalus, whose father made him a pair of wings. Ignoring instructions,
Icarus flew too close to the sun; the wax holding the feathers together melted, and
he fell into the sea.
12 The bishop has been tentatively identified as either St. Gregory of Nazianzus
(329–389 CE) or St. Nicholas of Bari (270–343 CE).

in a show of its origin,
carries the message: *pulvis es*,[13]

and sends you a true affection,
and seeing you are a wonder
of beauty, presumes that by a
miracle the Saint fashioned you.

This gift, being insufficient,
bears a likeness to its owner;
for an ancient proverb blesses
the one who resembles her own.[14]

This is the reason, señora,
it comes so fearful and submissive
that I think that Amor himself
hid it away, fully concealed.

Until this gift is duly assessed,
it remains so mute and noiseless
that even the wheels of the hand
mill keep and maintain the secret.[15]

---

13 Drinking occurs on a feast day, but in contrast, the gift of chocolate is in pow-
dered form, used for preparing a beverage. *Pulvis es* ("Thou art dust") is said on Ash
Wednesday by the priest as he draws a cross on the forehead of each worshiper.
14 The proverb states "Honor to those who resemble their families."
15 The reference is to the hand mill in which the chocolate was ground to powder.

Because the one who it is wants
you to know there is a Cupid,
making Amor a true calling,
for you are as fair as Psyche,

but not to know who he may be:
for it would be a foolish whim,
when snubbed for insufficiency,
to boast of how splendid he is.[16]

I must serve you, and so I know
in serving I do not oblige,
nor make a present of a debt
nor find service in repayment.

Since you do not know who I am,
I am inclined to brevity,
for a face loses character
when the mouth is firmly closed.

That is how I plan to keep it;
because I only reduce the
vanity of adoring you
in the glory of serving you.

16 The owner of the gift and the gift itself are definitively identified, though Sor
Juana insists on the anonymity of the giver—that is, Galve. It is assumed that the
ballad was written at the beginning of the Galve viceregency.

REDONDILLAS

(The *redondilla* is a stanza of four octosyllabic
lines, usually rhymed *abab*.)

My wish, Feliciana, is to
sing your celebrated beauty;
and since it is to be sung,
you will be the instrument.

About your ornamented head
my love says, with no misgiving,
that the high notes of your tresses
are in a harmony so fair

that with some audacity
love proclaims in a gentle voice
that he knows how to arrange them,
and his touch alone will strum them.

You must allow love to attempt
to configure the clefs and notes
from the expanse of your forehead
to the ruling lines of your brows.

At the music stand that occupies
your countenance, your eyes sing
re, mi, fa, sol to the rhythmic
tempo and measure of your nose.

The harmonious carnation
on your face is not discordant,
because along with the lily
it tempers and tunes your fair hue.

Your miraculous discretion
harmonizes with your beauty,
but the wisest, most prudent word
stammers if it touches your lip.

Your throat is the part that provides
the singing with inventions,
because of the diatonic
sequences that it crowds in.

You conquer the hearts of all
with your own sovereign command
for in your hand you sustain
the signs and the inclinations.

I shall not play the slenderness
of your fine, exquisite torso
for the bend of your waist is as
troubling as a trill in the song.

Upon your foot my hope places
all its pleasures and delights,

for since it does not go higher
it never makes a mutation.

And although it does not dare
to rise in plainsong, on pitch,
when counterpoint is adjoined
it emblazons the whole note.

Your body, its rhythm framed
from proportion to persistence,
creates a divine harmony,
it is so finely composed.

I shall be silent, for my love
does not interpret you well
in crude songs; to your perfections
you alone know the notation.

Begging pardon for her silence, on the occasion of breaking a precept to maintain it

I wish to beg your forgiveness,
señora, for my silence, if what
was intended as courtesy
makes it seem ill-bred instead.

And you cannot reprehend me
if my behavior until now
has been so concerned with loving
that it forgot to explain.

For in my amorous passion
it was not neglect or waning
to take from my tongue its speech
and give it instead to my heart.

Nor did I cease to invoke you;
because, as this passion of mine
could see you here in my soul,
here in my soul it spoke to you.

And in this notable idea
it lived felicitous, content,

for I could feign and pretend
that you looked on me with favor.

With so bizarre a design
did my useless hope survive;
for thinking of you as divine,
it could make you human again.

Oh how mad I saw myself
in the ecstasy of your love,
when even pretended your favors
could make me mad with delight!

Oh how, in your beautiful sun,
my ardent love set ablaze,
enflamed and fed by your brilliance,
it forgot about the dangers.

Forgive me if it was boldness
to dare approach your pure ardor,
for there is no holy place safe
from blameworthy lapses of thought.

It was in this manner that my
crazed hope deceived and deluded,
and deep inside me I had
all the good I did desire.

But now my mute silence breaks
your precept, severe and stern,
for it alone could be the key
to my adoration and praise.

And although loving your beauty
is a crime without a pardon,
let me be punished for the fault
rather than for indifference.

Do not, then, rigorous lady,
wish the one who declared her love
to be in truth unfortunate
when she had been joyful in jest.

If you condemn my irreverence,
condemn your power as well,
for if my obedience is wrong,
your command was not a just one.

If my intent is culpable,
my affection is ever damned,
because loving you is a crime
for which I shall never atone.

I find this in my affections,
and more I cannot explain;
but you, from what I did not say
will infer what I do not say.

REDONDILLA 92

She proves the inconsistency in the pleasure and censure of men who
accuse women of what they themselves cause

O foolish men who accuse
women with so little cause,
not seeing you are the reason
for the very thing you blame:

for if with unequaled longing
you solicit their disdain,
why wish them to behave well
when you urge them on to evil?

You contend with their resistance,
then say gravely that the conquest
arose from their licentiousness
and not your extreme diligence.

The audacity of your mad
belief resembles that of the
child who devises a monster
and then afterward fears it.

With foolish presumption you wish
to find the woman you seek,
for your mistress, a Thais,
and Lucretia for your wife.

Whose caprice can be stranger than
the man who ignores good counsel,
clouds the looking glass himself,
then complains it is not clear.

You occupy the same place
whether favored or disdained,
complaining if women are cruel
and mocking them if they love.

You think highly of no woman,
no matter how modest: if she
rejects you she is ungrateful,
and if she accepts, unchaste.

Always foolish in your actions,
with a measure that is uneven

you condemn one for being cruel,
another for being easy.

Then how can the woman you woo
be temperate toward your courting?
Ungrateful, she offends you,
and if easy, she angers.

But between anger and sorrow
the object of your caprice,
may be one who does not love you,
and then you may truly complain.

To their sorrow your lovers give
wings to restraints; they fly away,
and after you make them sinful
you wish they were filled with virtue.

Who carries the greater guilt
in a passion gone astray:
the woman, beseeched, who falls,
or the man who begged her to yield?

Or which one merits more blame
although both deserve our censure:
the woman who sins for pay,
or the man who pays to sin?

But why are you so alarmed
by the guilt you plainly deserve?
Love them for what you make them
or make them what you can love.

Cease your incessant entreaties,
and then, with justification,
you can accuse the affection
of the one who solicits you.

But I conclude your audacity
does battle with countless weapons,
for in promises and pleading
you join world, and flesh, and devil.

EPIGRAMS

EPIGRAM 93

A satirical lesson for one who is vain about her beauty

You say, Leonor, for beauty
you should be given the palm;
the one for virgin is better,
and this your face guarantees.
    Do not boast with such insolence
that you steal the heart of each man:
if you have been given the palm,
it is, Leonor, for bogeyman.[1]

EPIGRAM 94

In which she discovers the honorable lineage of a highborn drunkard

So that your blood may be known
you tell everyone, Alfeo,
you come from kings; I believe
you are of very fine stock,
    and that you anger all you meet
with your talk about those kings,

---

1 The pun is based on dual meanings for *palma* and *coco*. The first is both a palm tree and the equivalent of victory laurels; the second is both a coconut and a bogeyman used to frighten children.

who, more than the kings of swords,

must have been the kings of cups.[2]

EPIGRAM 95

Which provides a proud man with the eyewash he deserves[3]

Not having an upright father

would be a defect, in my eyes,

if I had chosen him, as I

received my being from him.

Your mother was more merciful,

for she made you heir of many,

so that among them all, you can

take the one who suits you best.[4]

2 Swords and cups are two of the suits in the Spanish deck (*baraja*), which is similar to the tarot deck.
3 Eyewash or collyrium, a traditional treatment for diseases of the eye. The implication is that the man needs to be cured of the ailment that allows him to see other people's defects, but not his own.
4 Sor Juana was born out of wedlock. The epigram seems to be a response to someone who criticized her for her birth.

Some moral advice to a modern captain

> Don Juan is a captain now:
> but my mind would much prefer
> for him to be more reformed[5]
> and a little less the captain.
>   For truly it perturbs me,
> in so venturesome an action,
> to see him not govern the bridle,
> and dare to use the short stirrup.

EPIGRAM 97

Which reveals to a sergeant the conditions he does not possess

> A certain sergeant armed himself
> with a victorious halberd;[6]
> but then he and she ended up
> as what I shall tell you now:

---

5 The pun is based on the dual meanings of *reformado*: "cashiered," in the military sense, and "reformed," in the moral sense.
6 A halberd is a medieval weapon consisting of an axe blade at the top of a long pole.

an "a" disappears from her,[7]
and she becomes a packsaddle;
his "sar" turns into the mange,
and the silver does not appear.

7 In Spanish the halberd is *alabarda*; if an "a" is removed, it becomes *albarda*, or packsaddle. Sergeant in Spanish is *sargento*; *sarna* is mange; *argento* is silver.

DÉCIMAS

❦

(A décima is a stanza of ten octosyllabic
lines. Rhyme schemes can vary, but the
rhyme itself is usually consonant.)

Which accompanied a portrait sent to a certain person

She who is my original
has forwarded me to you,
and although you see her drawn,
you will never see her withdrawn;
completely transformed in me,
she hands you the conquest: her love;
do not wonder at the calm
and silence you find in me:
my original, for your sake,
I believe has lost her soul.

Envious of my arrival,
and seeing in my good fortune
how she feels woe and sadness
and I, not feeling, have great luck.
I am doubtless attended by
a far more advantageous sign,
a far more favorable star;
for I was born of a paintbrush,
and had less life in my being
than she, but much more good fortune.

If by chance my lot were to change
and you wounded me, in order
not to see you do not love me
I would wish to be without life.
For the fact of being unloved
would be an event so dire,
the strength of that anguish would force
me, although painted, to feel:
for pain knows how to instill
souls in order to have feeling.

And if it is inopportune
for you that I lack a soul,
in me you can instill one
of the many you have captured:
for since I gave her soul to you,
and my being names itself yours,
although you are amazed to see
me in such insentient calm,
you are the soul of this body,
and the body of this shadow.

She depicts her respectful love; she speaks to the portrait and is not
silent as it is twice her master

Divine copy in which I see
the paintbrush presume, arrogant
when it sees that it has gone
where my desire could not go;
a high, sovereign use and mastery
of a more than human talent
free of impertinent boldness,
for your incredible beauty,
since it goes past what is possible,
cannot be reached even by thought.

What paintbrush was so supreme
that it sufficed to copy you?
What muse inspired and moved its mind?
What virtue guided its hand?
Let the futile art that shaped you
so perfectly not boast of this;
to form your beauty, a portent,
it was agreed and all concurred
that the instrument was human,
but the prompting impulse, divine.

I so wonder at you as spirit,
believe in you as deity,
that I find your unseen soul
and doubt the body I see:
I abrogate all my reason,
filled with wonder at your beauty
displayed with such reality,
and leaving the judgment serene
that even the soul is copied,
and the deity is seen.

Seeing the height of perfection
that I look upon in you,
then I scarcely can believe
that any can equal you;
and if there were no original
whose rare, unwonted perfection
had found its copy in you,
then I, a second Pygmalion,
and lost in fondness of you,
would implore that you come to life.

I touch you to see whether a
hidden life appears in you;
can it possibly be lacking
in what steals away my judgment?
Can you possibly not feel

this hand that caresses you
and incites you to attend
to my devoted, humble spoils?
Can there be no light in those eyes,
can there be no voice in that mouth?

I well can voice my complaint
when you calmly leave me alone
that you steal away my soul
yet still do not come to life;
and when, pitiless, you trample
my humility so proudly,
thereby purifying my pain,
your mercy moves so far away
that I lose my poor complaint
and torment is all that remains.

At times I think that, merciful,
you respond to my devotion;
and at others my heart fears
that, disdainful, you refrain.
Now joyful, my bosom takes heart,
now downcast at harshness, it dies,
but either way it acquires
the good fortune of possession,
for in the end, in my power,
you will be whatever I wish.

Although, faithful, you display the
harshness of your original,
the paintbrush has granted to me
what love cannot and never could.
I live, blissful in the favor
that a cold bronze offers to me,
for although you show indifference
and, at your worst, may say
you are unfeeling, never can
you declare, that you are not mine.

She points out the lucid profundity of an eminent orator

Spanish Cicero: my pen can
barely laud on seeing you,
for wishing to praise you means
presuming to understand you,
although one who gives ear to you
comes to know your discernment is
so vast it can cause dismay;
and so in your great subtlety
one knows there is lofty grandeur
but cannot measure the amount.

You are a sea that everyone
can contemplate but not fathom,
can marvel at when they see it,
but no one can ever sound;
when one comes to admire it,
from its great expanse one only
can infer its immensity:
for if by what can be seen
of the surface one is amazed,
what is the effect of the depths?

And although what I can see
fills me with vast admiration,
I know full well its perfection
cannot be fully encompassed
but, since I cannot understand
so much greatness, or encompass
the very thing I am hearing,
boldly I venture to praise it:
what I can grasp, with my reason;
what I cannot, with my faith.

*She comments in verse on the excuses of one who refused to
speak in prose*

The offense of being silent
you have attempted to excuse,
and you are much more convincing
in the things that you have said:
I have weighed and judged the offense
by your own clear declaration,
for one who speaks with this kind
of discretion quite clearly shows
that being silent was merely
a desire, not necessity.

When you excuse with discretion
the reason you remained silent,
you remind me of the loss
of all that you failed to say:
you increase for me the sorrow
I felt on the day I saw you
because then I could not hear you;
for proceeding with that silence,
I could neither weigh nor judge
the very thing I had lost.

To a discerning and valiant captain

Your plumes, I infer, are a sign
of bravery and discernment
but I cannot decide whether
for your helmet or your inkwell.
In your crest is' clearly displayed
a well-armed discernment joined
to a well-lettered bravery,
and to summarize I say
your blade cut and sharpened your quill,
your quill measures and scans your blade.

1 The plumes in the crest on the helmet of an officer could indicate his status as a soldier and a writer.

*For herself she refuses the liberty she begs of the Vicereine[2] for
an Englishman*

Today I bow at your feet
with the requisite deference,
I worship you as a god
and entreat you as a god.
Do not say I deny you
your rite, seeking the benefit
of your favor and protection,
for to the principal god,
invoking her favor and grace
is the most pleasing sacrifice.

Samuel appeals to your mercy,
pleading in various ways,
for he seeks to find his freedom
where everyone loses theirs.
Release him from his slavery,
señora, the reasons are just
and clement toward such ill fortune,

2 Starting in 1680, the vicereine of Mexico was María Luisa, Countess of Paredes,
married to the viceroy, the Marquis de la Laguna.

and at some time emancipate
all of those you have made captive.

In conflict my will here strives
for two contrary desires:
for the Englishman, liberty,
and for myself, to be your slave,
although I was born unworthy
of your giving me that name,
surely you will resist in vain
the marker of my slavery,
for I am bound to be yours
although you do not accept me.

The two petitions are contrary
if you peruse them with care,
for one aspires to liberty
and I yearn to be confined;
but your discernment, keen-sighted,
never impeded by doubt,
can, if it gauges intentions,
bring joy to us both today
by acceding to what I bring
and conceding to what he begs.

SONNETS

SONNET 145

In which she attempts to refute the praises of a portrait of the poet,
signed by truth, which she calls passion

This thing you see, a bright-colored deceit,
displaying all the many charms of art,
with false syllogisms of tint and hue
is a cunning deception of the eye;

this thing in which sheer flattery has tried
to evade the stark horrors of the years
and, vanquishing the cruelties of time,
to triumph over age and oblivion,

is vanity, contrivance, artifice,
a delicate blossom stranded in the wind,
a failed defense against our common fate;

a fruitless enterprise, a great mistake,
a decrepit frenzy, and rightly viewed,
a corpse, some dust, a shadow, mere nothingness.

SONNET 146

She complains of her adverse fortune, suggests her aversion to vice,
and justifies her diversion with the Muses

O World, why do you wish to persecute me?
How do I offend you, when I intend
only to fix beauty in my intellect,
and never my intellect fix on beauty?

I do not set store by treasures or riches;
and therefore it always brings me more joy
only to fix riches in my intellect,
and never my intellect fix on riches.

I do not set store by a lovely face that,
vanquished, is civil plunder of the ages,
and perfidious wealth has never pleased me,

for I deem it best, as one of my truths,
to deplete the vanities of this life
and never this life to deplete in vanities.

SONNET 147

In which she morally censures a rose, and thereby all that resemble it

O rose divine, in gentle cultivation
you are, with all your fragrant subtlety,
tuition, purple-hued, to loveliness,
snow-white instruction to the beautiful;

intimation of a human structure,
example of gentility in vain,
in whose one being nature has united
the joyful cradle and the mournful grave;

how haughty in your pomp, presumptuous one,
how proud when you disdain the threat of death,
then, in a swoon and shriveling, you give

a withered vision of a failing self;
and so, with your wise death and foolish life,
in living you deceive, dying you teach!

SONNET 148

She prefers to die rather than expose herself to the indignities of old age

Celia[1] looked at a rose that in the meadow
so happily displayed vain pomp and show,
and with creams of scarlet and crimson paint
gaily drenched and daubed her lovely face;

and Celia said: "Enjoy with no fear of fate
the too brief course of this your flowering youth,
for never can the death that comes tomorrow
take away from you the joy of today;

and even though death hurries and hastens near
and fragrant life leaves and abandons you,
do not lament your dying so fair and young:

remember—the wisdom of the world will say
you were fortunate to die while beautiful
and not endure the indignity of age."

---

1 Celia is a frequent name in the pastoral tradition.

She earnestly recommends the choice of a condition that lasts
until death

If one considered the dangers of the sea,
one would never set sail; if the hazard were
clearly seen, no one would dare to provoke
the attack of a brave, undaunted bull;

if the prudent rider pondered the bolting
fury of a spirited galloping beast,
never would anyone bring it to a halt
with an able hand controlling the reins.

But if there were someone valiant enough
that, despite the danger, he would attempt
to drive with daring hand the swift chariot

bathed in light of great Apollo himself,
he might do all this but never enter
a state that must last the rest of his life.

Green[2] rapture and delight of human life,
crazed Hope, in delirious gilded frenzy,
the intricate sleep of those who are awake,
as bereft of treasures as it is of dreams;

soul of the world, exuberant old age,
and then decrepit verdancy imagined;
of the favored the long awaited today,
and of the less fortunate, the tomorrow:

let those with green lenses before their eyes,
seeing all things painted to their desire,
follow your shadow, in search of your day;

for I, wiser, more prudent in my fortune,
hold in both of my hands both of my eyes,
and see no more than those things I can touch.

2 Green is traditionally the color of hope. Today we would speak of rose-colored glasses.

In which she responds to jealous suspicion with the rhetoric of weeping

This afternoon, my love, when I spoke to you,
I could see in your face, in what you did,
that you were not persuaded by mere words,
and I wished you could see into my heart;

and Love,[3] assisting me in my attempt,
overcame the seeming impossible,
for among the tears that my sorrow shed
was my breaking heart, liquid and distilled.

Enough of anger now, my love, enough;
do not let tyrant jealousy torment you,
nor base suspicion roil your serenity

with foolish specters and deceptive clues;
in liquid humor[4] you have seen and touched
my broken heart and held it in your hands.

3 The reference is to the classical god of love.
4 Humor here refers to a bodily fluid.

SONNET 165

Which restrains a fantasy by making it content with decent love

Halt, O faint shade of my elusive love,
image of the enchantment I love best,
fair illusion for whom I gladly die,
sweet fiction for whose sake I live in pain.

If th'attraction, the magnet of your charms
draws my heart as if it were made of steel,
why woo and win me over with flattery
if then you will deceive me, turn and flee?

But, satisfied and proud, you cannot boast
that your tyranny triumphs over me:
for though you escape and slip through the tight cords

that bind your imagined form in fantasy,
it matters not if you elude my arms,
my dear, when thought alone can imprison you.

The very distressing effects of love, but no matter how great, they do not equal the qualities of the one who causes them

Do you see me, Alcino,[5] here am I caught
in the chains of love, shackled in its irons,
a wretched slave despairing of her freedom,
and so far, so distant from consolation?

Do you see my soul filled with pain and anguish,
wounded by torments so savage, so fierce,
burned in the midst of living flames and judging
herself unworthy of her castigation?

Do you see me without a soul, pursuing
a folly I myself condemn as strange?
Do you see me bleeding along the way

as I follow the trail of an illusion?
Are you very surprised? See then, Alcino:
the cause of harm to me deserves much more.

5 Standard name used in pastoral poetry of the Golden Age.

SONNET 177

She reflects upon her inevitable weeping in view of the one she loves

You command me, Anarda,[6] to come without
weeping before your eyes, and I suspect
that not knowing the cause is what has made you
wish me to undertake so great a triumph.

Love, my lady, finds in me no resistance,
for my exhausted heart he sets ablaze,
causing the blood in my bosom to flee
and vaporize in my sight as ardency.

And then my eyes seek and search for your presence,
which they judge the object of their sweet charm,
and when my attention pays homage to you

the rays from my eyes, during all that time,
finding in you the resistance of snow,
transmute what left as vapor into tears.

6 Standard name used in pastoral poetry of the Golden Age.

Which explains the most sublime quality of love

I adore Lisi[7] but do not pretend
that Lisi will return my token of love,
for if I deem her beauty within reach,
I offend both her honor and my mind.

To intend nothing is all my intention;
for I know that to merit so much grandeur
no merit can suffice, and it is foolish
to act contrary to my understanding.

I conceive her great beauty as something so
sacred that audacity does not wish
to give the slightest opening to hope:

for yielding my great happiness to hers,
in order not to see it badly used,
I think I would regret seeing her mine.

7 Lisi, or Lysi, is a standard name used in pastoral poetry of the Golden Age.

Convalescing from a serious illness, she addresses the Vicereine,
Señora Marquesa de Mancera, attributing to her great love her
improvement even in dying

In this life of mine that ever was yours,
O divine Laura, and ever will be,
the savage Fate, determined to pursue me,
wanted to claim my mortal foot in triumph.

I was astounded by her rash daring,
for if great power lies 'neath her domain,
she no longer can wield any in mine:
you allowed me to free myself from her.

I saw the mortal, fearsome scissors open
to cut through the thread she never had spun;
oh savage, terrible Fate! I said then,

know that no one but Laura commands here;
and she, abashed, departed and sped away,
leaving me to die for you, no one but you.

SONNET 187

On the death of the most excellent Señora Marquesa de Mancera

The heavens, enamored of the comeliness
of Laura, stole her away, took her on high,
for it did not seem correct to illumine
these unhappy valleys in that pure light;

or because mere mortals, deceived, misguided
by the beauteous structure of her body,
astonished at the sight of extreme beauty,
did not consider themselves as fortunate.

She was born where the east draws a scarlet veil
at the rising of the rubicund star,
and she died where, with burning, ardent desire,

the depths of the sea swallows that red light;
for it was needed for her divine flight
that like the sun she travel around the world.

SONNET 188

On the same subject

A beautiful merging severed in Laura,
O immortal soul, O glorious spirit,
why did you leave a body so beauteous
and why to that soul have you bid farewell?

But now it has penetrated my reason
that you endure so rigorous a divorce
so that on the last day you can with joy
once again become eternally joined.

Begin your rapid flight, O fortunate soul,
and released now from your beauteous prison,
leaving its rosy hue turned into ice,

rise up to be crowned by luminous stars:
for all of boundless heaven is required
so that you will not miss your beauteous home.

SONNET 189

Because you have died, Laura, let affections
die too that yearn, desiring you in vain,
along with these eyes you deprive of the sight
of the beautiful light you once bestowed.

And let my forlorn lyre die, where you inspired
echoes that mournfully cry out for you,
and let even these ill-favored strokes become
the black tears of my melancholy pen.

Then let Death herself be moved to take pity,
who was compelled and could not pardon you;
and let Love lament his own bitter fate,

for if at one time, he longed to enjoy you
and wished to have eyes so that he could see you,
now they will serve him only to weep for you.

She applauds the astronomical science of Father Eusebio Francisco
Quino, of the Company of Jesus,[8] *who wrote of the comet that appeared*
in the year 1680, declaring it free of portents

Although the pure light of heaven is bright,
and bright is the moon and the stars are bright,
and bright the ephemeral lightning streaks
that the air raises and fire consumes;

although the thunderbolt is bright, whose harsh
production costs the wind a thousand disputes,
and the lightning flash that made of its tracks
a fearsome light in the ebony dark;

all of our human knowledge, dim and slow,
lay in darkness without our mortal feathers
able to be, in proud and boastful flight,

another Icarus of reasoned discourse,
until you, O sovereign Eusebio,
shed light upon the very lights of heaven.

---

8 Company of Jesus was the name used by St. Ignatius Loyola, the founder of the
Jesuit order. Society of Jesus came into use subsequently as a translation of the
Latin document authorizing the establishment of the order.

FIRST DREAM

꙰

(Like Góngora's *The Solitudes*, this is written
in the random alternation of seven- and
eleven-syllable lines called a *silva*.)

as titled and composed by Mother Juana Inés de la Cruz, in imitation of
Góngora

Pyramidal, funereal, a shadow
born of earth, aspiring to highest heaven,
the haughty tip of its great obelisks
striving in vain to climb up to the stars,
and yet their resplendent light
(sparkling always, always unassailable)
from their great height scoffed at and
mocked the gloom of the war
waged on them with black vapors
by fearsome, ephemeral
shadows, whose dark glower could not reach even
the outer convexity of the sphere
of the thrice comely goddess
who shows us a trio of fair visages;[1]
could master no more than mere
air that misted in the rush
of thick dense breath exhaled by that grim shadow;
and in the contained stillness
of the soundless empire
only muffled voices of nocturnal birds
were countenanced and approved,
so obscure, so serious,

---

1 In classical mythology, Selene had three faces: Luna, or the moon in the sky,
Diana or Artemis on earth, and Persephone or Hecate in the underworld.

their calls did not unsettle the quietude.

Sluggish of flight, with a song

irksome to the ear, more so to the spirit,

a shamed Nyctymene lurks at

chinks and cracks in sacred doors

or the most propitious gaps in high lunettes

which may offer a breach to her intention

to reach, in sacrilege, the

bright sacred lamps of the eternal flame

and extinguish them, unless she defames them

first, consuming the dense oil

found in the cloudless liquid

that the fruit of the famed tree of Minerva[2]

gave up in anguished drops when cruelly pressed.

And those three maidens[3] who saw

their house turned to wasteland, their cloth to weeds,

for having disobeyed the divine Bacchus,

no longer recounting a mélange of tales,

they too have been turned into odious shapes,

forming a second haze,

fearing to be seen even in the shadows,

birds with wings but no feathers:

those three diligent maidens,

sisters, I say, too daring,

2 The reference is to the olive tree.
3 Three sisters in Thebes who stayed home weaving and telling one another stories instead of worshiping Bacchus; as punishment they were turned into bats.

received the dire punishment
of bare drab membranes for wings,
so ill disposed the most hideous birds do
mock them: they, with one who once
served as the long-tongued minister to Pluto
but now is superstitious sign to augurs,[4]
alone composed the fearsome
tuneless choir, intoning black *maximas*
and *longas,*[5] more with long pauses than voices,
waiting perhaps for greater proportion from
this dull, slow-moving measure
than from the phlegmatic motion of the wind,
whose rhythm was so dilatory, so slack,
it may have slept between strokes.
This, then, melancholy, intercadent sound
from the fearsome, shadowed crowd
attracted attention less
than it moved one to slumber;
but first, so laggardly, its
consonance sluggish and dull
induced one to quiet rest
and invited all one's limbs to calm repose;

---

4 Ascalaphus told Pluto that Persephone had eaten part of a pomegranate, thereby
obliging her to spend half the year in the underworld. As punishment she turned
him into a horned owl.

5 These are terms used in mensural notation, the system of musical notation com-
mon in Europe from the thirteenth to the seventeenth centuries.

suggesting utter silence to the living,
silent dark Harpocrates, the night, seals
lips, one after the other
with an indicant finger,
to whose imperious, but not harsh, precept
each deferred, obedient.
Serene the wind now, the dog quiet in sleep,
one lies still, the other hushed;
not even atoms moving,
fearing the faint murmurous sound might make a
noise, sacrilegious though slight,
to violate the silent tranquility.
The sea, no longer perturbed,
did not even rock the unstable cradle,
cerulean blue, where the sun sinks to sleep;
and the fish, forever mute, slumbering deep
in the muddied beds of their
lightless, cavernous grottoes
were rendered now doubly mute;
and among them the deceitful enchantress
Almone,[6] who once had changed
simple lovers into fish,
here changed as well, now revenged.
In the hidden concave hollows of the high
mountains, those rough and cragged peaks

6 A Naiad in Ovid's *Metamorphoses*.

guarded less by ruggedness
than by their obscurity,
in whose dark, somber dwelling
deepest night reigns at midday,
and unknown still to the sure,
steady, tracking foot of the expert hunter,
forgotten the fierceness of
some, the terror of others,
the lowly animals slept,
paying to Nature the same
universal tribute imposed by her might;
and their king,[7] affecting vigilance, even
with open eyes kept no watch.
A powerful monarch[8] once,
torn to pieces by his own fierce hunting dogs
but now a timorous hart
with hearing most attentive
to the least perceptible tremor that may
disturb the atoms, first one
then the other of his sharp ears responds, moves
and quivers and hears the sound
even in his deep slumber.
And in the serene quietude of their nests,
hammocks formed of offshoots

---

7 The lion, king of the animals.
8 Actaeon saw Artemis and her nymphs bathing and was turned into a stag that
was then torn to pieces by his hunting dogs.

in the densest, most opaque parts of the trees,
the buoyant throng gathers together and sleeps,
the wind resting in the cessation of the
constant cutting of their wings.
The noble bird of Jupiter,[9] highborn queen,
does not give herself to rest
entirely, deeming sleep in excess vice,
and takes care to avert faults
of omission caused by lack of vigilance,
resting her entire weight on just one foot
and clutching in the other a tiny stone,
an alarm calculated to waken her
in the event she drowses:
for if a light sleep proves beyond her control
it would not last but be interrupted first
by regal or rather pastoral care.
Oh heavy burden and cost of majesty,
which does not forgive the least neglect or slip!
The reason, perhaps, that the crown is circular,
a mysterious gold circle that denotes
a no less unbroken zeal.
In short, all was possessed by sleep; all, in short,
was occupied by silence:
even the thief lay sleeping,
and even the watchful lover closed his eyes.

9 The eagle.

Dead of night[10] had almost passed, the darkness half
concluded, when wearied by their daily tasks,
(and oppressed not only by
grueling physical labor but tired too
of delight, since any constant incidence,
no matter how delightful,
also exhausts the senses:
for nature always alternates,
moves between first one, then the other scale,
allotting actions to leisure and labor
in the alternation, faithful unfaithful,
with which she guides the great machine of the world);
the limbs, then, occupied by sweet, profound sleep,
the senses, if not deprived
of their usual pursuit (work after all,
yet work well loved if
toil's ever lovable)
then suspended for a time,
and ceding to the image contrary to
life[11] that, slowly armed, cowardly charges and then
lazily conquers all with drowsing weapons,
from the lowly staff to the haughty scepter,
no distinction made between
coarse wool and the purple royal:

10 Midnight.
11 The imagery here and in the following lines is based on the traditional equiva-
lence of sleep and death.

for the leveler of sleep, all powerful,
grants privilege to none, not
the one whose sovereign tiara is formed
by three crowns,[12] nor the one who
dwells in a hovel of straw;
not the one whose golden hue
comes from the surging Danube,[13]
nor one who with humble reed builds his poor hut;
with an ever equal rod
Morpheus (that powerful image of death)
measures the roughest cloth, the finest brocade.
The soul, then, unburdened of
external rule that holds sway when, occupied
by material concerns, for good or ill
she spends the day, remote now
but not completely apart,
only confers wages of vegetative
warmth to languid limbs and tranquil bones oppressed
by that passing death, for the body serene
is like a corpse with a soul,
dead to life, alive to death,
the vital balance wheel of the human clock[14]
proffers scant signs of living,
if not with hands then arterial concord,

12 The Pope.
13 The Holy Roman Emperor.
14 The heart.

a few small proofs beating a measured display
of its well-ordered movement.
This member, then, the king and living center
of the vital spirits, with
its companion, a breathing
bellows (the lung that like a magnet attracts
air in never uneven movements, either
constricting or expanding
the conduit, muscular yet clear and soft,
making it breathe in the cool surrounding air
that it exhales when heated,
and the air avenges its expulsion by
committing small thefts of our natural warmth[15]
at some time wept for but never recovered,
and if not felt now, call no
theft small when oft repeated):
these then, I say, exceptions, each a truthful
witness, safeguarded that life,
while with muted voices, silent, the senses
impugned their testimony,
no reply their only proof,
as did the tongue, slowed and dull,
refuting them as it could no longer speak.
And that most able scientific workshop[16]

15 The imagery in this passage suggests that the fact of living brings us closer
to death.
16 The stomach.

a skilled and provident dispenser of heat
to other members never
a miser, ever active, not preferring
the nearer part or forgetting the removed,
and on a just, natural quadrant making
note of the portion each member should receive
of the chyle,[17] that constant heat distilled from food
which, merciful mediator, interposed
its innocent substance between that heat and
the radical moisture, paying full price
for the compassion, perhaps the arrogance,
the inane foolhardiness
that exposed it to a voracious rival,
a punishment deserved, even if excused
for one who intervenes in
the dispute of another:
this, if no forge of Vulcan,
then a temperate fire of human heat
that transmitted to the brain
the damp but most clear vapors
of the four tempered humors[18]

---

17 A fluid formed in the small intestine during digestion.
18 A balance among the four humors (blood, phlegm, black bile, and yellow bile)
was considered necessary for good health. The physiology in this section (the
relationship among intellect, imagination, memory, and fantasy) is Aristotelian
and Scholastic.

that not only did not cloud the semblances
the intellect gave to imagination
which, for safer keeping and in purer form,
presented them to diligent memory
that etched them, tenacious, and guards them with care,
but permitted fantasy
to form diverse images. And just as on
the untroubled surface, crystalline portent
of Pharos, that uncommon refuge and port,
in the quicksilver mirror
at vast distances one sees clearly almost
all the realm of Neptune, despite the expanse,
and the far-off ships that furrowed it, the size,
number, and fortune of bold vessels risked on
a shifting, transparent field,
while their light sails and weighty keels divided
waters and blustering winds:
so did serene fantasy
copy images of all things, the unseen
brush shaping, without light, bright mental colors,
the figures not only of all sublunar
creatures but also of those
clear hues that are intellectual stars
and in the manner that the invisible
can be conceived, ingeniously represents
and displays them to the Soul.

She, meanwhile, transformed into
immaterial being and beautiful
essence, contemplated that
spark shared with highest Being and cherished it
deep inside, in His image;
and deeming herself almost separated
from the coarse corporeal chain[19] that keeps her
ever bound, hinders the flight of intellect
that measures the immensity of the sphere,
or ponders the predictable orbits of
diverse heavenly bodies
the study of astrology, however,
a serious fault, the deserved punishment,
(severe contortion of tranquility)
of a uselessly judicial study[20]
then placed, it seemed to her, upon the highest
peak of a mountain that Atlas,
the giant presiding over all others,
deferred to as if a dwarf
and Olympus that never
permitted an agitated soft breeze to
violate the serenity of its brow
could not be called its foothill;
for the clouds, an opaque crown

19 The body that confines the soul.
20 Judicial astrology, or the prediction of future events, was condemned by the
Church in the Middle Ages and Renaissance.

on the highest mass of stone,
the haughtiest volcano,
which like a giant reaches up from the earth
declares war on the sky,
are hardly a dense part of
its proud height, and on its vast
waist they are a mere rough cord that, badly tied,
is undone by the surly wind
or drained by the heat of the proximate sun.
The first region of its loft
(the lowest part, I mean to say, dividing
its fearsome sheer height in three)
the swift flight of the eagle could not attain
(challenging the heavens and drinking the rays
of the sun, wishing to nest in that splendor),
now striving more than ever with all its strength,
now beating its two feathered sails, now raking
the air with its talons, struggling to break that
impunity with two wings,
weaving steps out of atoms.

The two pyramids (blazons
of vain Memphis, if not now flags fixed, unwaving,
a masterwork hard-wrought of architecture),
whose summit crowned with barbaric trophies, tomb
and banner to the Ptolemies, proclaimed to
the wind, to the clouds (if not heaven itself)

Egyptian glories, the great deeds of Memphis,
their proud, ever triumphant
city, called Cairo today,
for fame, struck dumb by the number, did not sing
that glory, those deeds, but they are imprinted
even in the wind, the sky;
these, whose height in graded symmetry rose
with so much tapering art
(as it mounted to the sky)
that the eye, no matter how keen, beheld it
vanish in the winds, unable to see the
subtle tip that appears to touch the first sphere[21]
until, wearied by wonder,
it did not descend but plunged,
found itself at the foot of the ample base,
scarcely recovered from vertigo, the harsh
retribution for winged, visual daring,
whose opaque bodies not opposed to the sun
but reconciled with its light, and if not
confederated (as, in effect, adjoined),
so completely bathed in its brilliance, so bright,
that to scorched travelers they
ne'er offered a small cover, a vestige of shade
for wearied breath or for weakening feet;
these, whether they be glories

21 The sphere of the moon.

of Egypt or profane pomp,

barbarous hieroglyphs of blind error,

according to the sweet Greek poet,[22] also

blind (because he writes the heroic feats of

Achilles, or the martial

subtleties of Ulysses, the learned guild

of historians does not admit him, or

accepts him when it counts him in its records

to swell these more by glory than by number),

it would be easier to take the blazing

bolt of lightning from the dreaded Thunderer[23]

or the heavy studded club from Alcides

than a single hemistich

from the countless series of sweet verses a

well-disposed Apollo dictated to him:

Following the maxim, I say, of Homer,

pyramids were mere material models,

are the intentional species of the soul,

as the ambitious flame burns upward in a

pyramidal tip toward heaven, so does the

human mind, miming that form,

ever aspire to the First Cause,[24]

the center toward which all straight lines extend, if

22 Homer.
23 Jupiter.
24 God.

not the circumference that holds,
infinite, all essences.

Then these two spurious mounts
(be they marvel, be they miracles)
and even that blasphemous haughty tower,[25]
its mournful remains today
not stones but discordant tongues
because voracious time does not consume them,
diverse idioms that render difficult
amicable conversance among peoples
(making those created as one by nature
seem different because their languages are strange),
if all of these were compared
to the sublime mental pyramid where the
soul was placed and saw herself, not knowing
how, they would be so diminished one would judge
the tip of that pyramid one of the spheres;
for the ambitious longing of the soul rose
higher than her own flight, placed part of her mind
on a soaring pinnacle,
so far above herself that she believed she
had left herself behind for a new region.
At that great, almost immeasurable height,

25 The Tower of Babel.

joyful but perplexed, perplexed
but resolute, amazed although resolute,
the queen, supreme sovereign[26] of the sublunar
world, freely cast the keen gaze
of her beautiful eyes of intellect, no
spyglass before them (without fear of distance,
or mistrust of obstacle,
or concealing object interposed), over
all creation, whose immense entirety,
incomprehensible accumulation,
appeared clear and possible
to the eye but not the understanding, which
(stunned by a glut of objects,
its power far exceeded by their grandeur)
retroceded, a coward.
And so a repentant eye revoked the goal,
so rash, to vainly boast of
a contest with an object whose excellence
exceeds the visual lines,
against the Sun, I say, the brilliant body
whose rays are fiery punishment, unequal
forces scorning they chastise,
ray by ray, the arrogant
challenge, presumptuous first, then lamented

26 The human soul.

(a foolish experiment
that proved so costly to Icarus[27] whose own
tears, compassionate, drowned him),
as the understanding here
vanquished as much by the immense multitude
(the weighty apparatus
of so many species comprised in a sphere)
as by the qualities of each, surrendered:
so awe-stricken that (placed in such profusion
and therefore impoverished by indifference
in a sea of marvels, its choices confused),
it was lost and almost foundered in the waves;
and looking at everything, nothing it saw,
and could not even discern
(the intellective faculty repelled by
so many diverse species,
so extensive, so incomprehensible,
which it gazed upon, from the axis, where the
whirling mechanism of the world rested,
to the antipodal pole)
the parts, now not only those
that all the universe deems
not trappings but perfections of ornament
but even the integrant,

27 Presented here as an example of unbridled ambition.

proportionally able
parts of its massive body.

But like one for whom prolonged obscurity
has usurped colors from visible objects,
if struck by sudden brilliance
is left more blind by the excess of the light
(for excess has the opposite effect on
a dulled, unaccustomed faculty that then
cannot bear light of the sun)
and against these offenses of the light,
one summons the darkness, once the gloomy
impediment to one's sight,
over and again, a hand
keeping vacillant rays from weak dazzled eyes,
shade, pious arbiter, now the instrument
of their recovery by
stages so that after they
perform more steadfastly their operation
a natural recourse, an innate knowledge
confirmed by experience,
mute teacher, perhaps, but worthy oratory
could persuade other Galens,[28]

28 Here, represents any doctor.

that from a fatal toxin, occult noxious
qualities might be measured in scrupulous
proportioned doses, whether for abundant
excess of heat or cold, or to affect the
unknown sympathies or antipathies by
which natural causes make their progress
course (displaying to astounded wonderment a
certain effect from an unknown cause, with
fecund sleeplessness and careful
empirical attention
examining brutes first to lessen danger),
the beneficial concoction was prepared,
highest goal of the Apollonian science,
an amazing antidote,
and so perhaps from evil can come great good:
in no other way did the soul, awestruck
at the sight of so vast an
object summon her attention that, scattered
by so much diversity
still could not recover from the portentous
awe that had calmed her discourse,
allowing only the formless embryo
of a confused concept which, so misshapen,
depicted in disordered chaos all the
blur of species it embraced,
come together with no order, come apart
with none, and the more they attempt to combine

the more they dissolve apart,
too filled with their difference,
encircling with violence the diffuseness
of so many objects in a container
so small, scant even for the least and lowest.
And so, sails furled, entrusted unwittingly
to a traitorous sea, disquieting wind
(seeking fidelity in a heedless sea
and constancy in the wind),
she anchored unwillingly
on the mental shore, chastened,
rudder destroyed, mast broken,
the ship-kissing sands of the beach with splinters,
where, now recovered, prudent
reflection usurped repairs, and circumspect
judgment replaced lack of thought:
and curbed in her actions she deemed it best to
reduce to a single theme,
or separately to examine
what can be reduced to the
two times five and ingenious categories:[29]
metaphysical reduction that teaches
(conceiving of general entities in
a few mental images

29 These are the ten Aristotelian categories indicating what can be predicated about something in a proposition. They are: substance, quantity, quality, relation, place, time, posture, having, action, and affection.

in which reason, abstracted, disdains matter)
how to form knowledge from universals,
correcting with forewarned art
the inability to grasp in only
one intuitive act all of creation,
but scaling a ladder, ascends, step by step,
from one concept to the next
and that of comprehending a relative
order, following, of necessity, the
limited vigor of the understanding
that bases its gains on successive discourse;
doctrine strengthens, with learned nourishment, her
feeble forces, and the lengthy, if clement,
continuing current of the discipline
instills a robust spirit so that boldly
she aspires to the glorious laurel
of the most arduous striving, and ascends
the high rungs, devoting herself first to one
then another faculty,
until immaterially she looks upon
the honorable summit,
the sweet conclusion of her arduous zeal
(bitterly sown, a fruit pleasing to the taste,
even her long fatigue a small price to pay)
and with valiant foot she trods
the soaring pinnacle of that lofty brow.

My understanding desired to follow
the method of this series,
that is, to pass from the lowest degree of
inanimate being (least favored if not
most unprotected of all produced by the
second cause[30]), to the nobler ranking that in
vegetal life is first born, although crude, of
Themis (the first who at her
fertile maternal breasts with
attractive virtue expressed
the sweet springs of terrestrial humor that
as natural sustenance is the sweetest food),
a ranking adorned by four
diverse, quite contrary acts,
which attracts, then diligently segregates
what it deems unsuitable,
expels the superfluous, and makes the most
useful substances its own;[31]
and (once investigated)
probes a more beautiful form
(adorned with senses and more
than senses apprehensive
imaginative power),
that with reason can give rise to a dispute,

30 That is, nature, created by God, the First Cause.
31 This passage describes the four operations of vegetative life, according to
Aristotle.

when not an insult to the inanimate
star that gleams and shines most bright
with haughty splendor, for the
lowest creature, the most humble can provoke
envy, possess advantage;[32]
and making of this bodily knowledge the
foundation, however meager, moves on to
the supreme, the marvelous, the tripartite
composite ordered of three harmonious
lines and of all lower forms
a mysterious recapitulation:[33]
the decisive joining of pure nature raised
to the heights, enthroned, and the
least noble, the most contemptible creature:[34]
adorned not only with the five faculties
of sense but ennobled by
the three directing internal ones,[35] the gift,
and not in vain, of a wise, powerful hand,
to be mistress of the rest:
the zenith of His works, the circle that joins
the sphere and earth, ultimate perfection of

32 These are the attributes of animals, according to Aristotle.
33 This passage describes human beings, "tripartite" because they incorporate
vegetative, sensitive, and rational elements.
34 Humans unite the physical materiality of the world with the spirituality of
the angels.
35 The three aspects of the soul: intellect, memory, and will.

creation and ultimate

delight of the Eternal Creator, and

in whom, satisfied, His vast magnificence

came to rest, portentous origination:

no matter how haughtily it reaches for

heaven, dust closes its mouth,

its mysterious image

might be the sacred vision that the Eagle

of the Evangels[36] saw in Patmos, which walked

among the stars and on earth with equal steps,

or the huge statue[37] whose rich high head of the

most precious metal was made,

its base of the most scorned and weakest substance,

shattered at the least motion:

man, I say, in short, the greatest wonder that

human understanding can devise, absolute

compendium that resembles the angels,

the plants, the brutes; whose exalted lowliness

partakes of all of nature.

Why? Perhaps because more fortunate than the

rest, it is elevated

by the grace of a loving union.[38] And oh,

36 The reference is to Saint John the Divine, who wrote the Book of Revelation.
37 Described in Daniel 2:31–33, the image dreamed by Nebuchadnezzar and interpreted by Daniel.
38 The reference is to the Incarnation.

grace, though repeated, never well enough known

as it seems to be ignored

so little valued and so unrequited!

These, then, were the steps I wished at times to take,

but at others I forswore

that wish, judging it excessive boldness

in one who failed to comprehend the smallest,

the most simple part of natural effects

nearest at hand, to attempt

to apprehend everything;

one who could not grasp the secret, obscure way

the pleasant fountain led its crystalline course,[39]

lingering, detained, in slow meanders, through

the fearsome bosom of Pluto, dire caverns

of the dreadful abyss, bright

tracker searching the smiling meadows, lovely

Elysian Fields, the nuptial

chamber of a triform wife

(useful curiosity, though wearisome,

for she gave a true account

of the beautiful daughter, unrecovered,

to the golden goddess who troubled mountains,

forests, questioned meadows, woods,

---

39 The fountain of the nymph Arethusa became a river that ran underground, through Hades and the Elysian Fields. She reported to Ceres (the "golden goddess") the whereabouts of her daughter Persephone (the "triform wife").

seeking her life but losing it in sorrow);
one who did not know why an ivory cast
circles the frail beauty of a brief flower:
why a mingling of colors, scarlet blending
with the whiteness of dawn, is
its fragrant finery, or
why it exhales the scent of amber, unfolds
to the wind its raiment, beauteous because
delicate, which multiplies
into countless new daughters, forming a frilled
display fringed with gold tracings
and, the white bud seal broken,
boastfully flaunts the plunder,
the sweet wound of the goddess of Cyprus[40] and,
if that which colors it did
not usurp the whiteness from dawn, the purple
from the break of day, blending
them into a purpled white,
a snowy russet: iridescent blossom
inciting the same applause from the meadow
that it solicits, perhaps
a tutor in vanities if not profane
exemplar of feminine skill that makes the
most active poison two times more venomous

40 Venus. In this passage the white and red of a flower and a woman's complexion
are compared, and the rose offers an argument against the use of cosmetics.

in the veil of appearance
of one who feigns a radiant complexion.
Then—my timid thought repeated—if before
a single object knowledge flees, and reason,
a coward, turns away; if before a lone
species deemed independent of the rest and
free of affiliation, understanding
turns its back and a frightened reason withdraws
from the difficult contest it refuses
to enter valiantly, for,
a coward, it fears it will understand it
badly, or never, or late,
how could it reflect on so fearsome and vast
a mechanism, its weight
terrible, unbearable if it did not
rest on its very center, enough to crush
the back of Atlas, even exceed the strength
of Alcides; would the one with sufficient
counterweight to the sphere judge the immense mass
less weighty, less ponderous
than the intent to investigate nature?

Other times, more fearless, it denounced as
too cowardly ceding the laurel even
before entering into harsh combat, and
turned to the bold example

of that illustrious youth,[41]

proud charioteer of the fiery coach,

his gallant if luckless high impulse firing

the spirit to the place where valor finds more

open paths of daring than fear encounters

examples of chastisement,

for once traveled, no punishment threatened

can halt a second attempt,

(second ambition, I say).

Neither deep mausoleum,

cerulean tomb for his unhappy ashes,

nor vengeful fulminating thunderbolt moves

despite its warning, an arrogant valor

that, despising life, resolves

to make his name eternal

in his own ruination.

Rather it is a model: a pernicious

example that engenders the wings for a

repeated flight of the ambitious spirit

that flatters terror itself

to compliment bravery,

spells glories among the letters of havoc.

Would that the punishment never be made known

so that the crime would never be attempted:

41 Phaethon, the son of Helios, the Sun (see page 21, n. 11). Here he becomes an example of daring for Sor Juana. The "cerulean tomb" refers to the Po River, where his body fell; the "thunderbolt" was used by Jupiter to kill him.

politic silence instead
as a circumspect ruler
might destroy the records of the case, either
simulating with feigned ignorance, or with
secret penalties punishing insolent
excess, not suggesting to popular view
a noxious example: word of the evil
of a great crime is its threat,
knowledge inciting extensive contagion;
for repeating a merely single crime would
be more remote among the ignorant than
among those who were cautioned.

But while choice foundered, confused, among the reefs,
touching sandbars of courses impossible
to follow each time it tried,
heat, finding nothing on which to feed, for its
temperate flame (a flame after all even
if temperate, for in its active mode it
consumes and well may inflame)
could not avoid transforming
its sustenance, turning the foreign matter
into its own substance: and the boisterous
boiling produced by the union of moisture
and heat in the wondrous natural vessel[42]

---

42 The stomach. This passage describes the slow awakening because an empty
stomach is no longer sending up to the brain the digestive vapors that cause sleep.

had ceased (lacking more fuel), and so the vapors
rising from it, damp, soporific hampered
the throne of reason (and from there sweet torpor
poured on the limbs) consumed by the mild ardor
of heat, unlocking the chains
of sleep: and the extended limbs feeling want
of food, weary of rest, not fully awake
nor asleep, signal desire for movement
with indolent stretches, slowly extending
benumbed nerves, and tired bones
(still without the entire will of their master)
returning to the other,
side, senses (so sweetly hindered by natural
henbane[43]) began to recover their powers
eyes opening and closing.
And from the mind, now idle,
the phantoms[44] fled and, as if of lightest
vapor, their form changed to evanescent smoke
and wind. As a magic lantern represents
diverse feigned and painted figures on a white
wall, assisted no less by shadow than by
light: maintaining in tremulous reflections
the distance mandated by
a learned perspective, the measurements

---

43 A natural soporific.
44 The images formed during sleep, as unreal as those projected on a wall by a
magic lantern.

verified in countless trials,
the fugitive shadow that vanishes in
splendor itself, feigns the form
of a body, adorned by all dimensions,
when it does not deserve to
be deemed even a surface.

Meanwhile the fiery father of light[45] knew
the fixed time had come to near the orient,
and he bade farewell to the opposite pole,
setting behind the mountains:
for the same point where his light in tremulous
swoons, meets their occident it
luminously adorns our orient.
But before that the beautiful, gentle star
of Venus cast the first light
with the beauteous wife of old Tithonus[46]
(an Amazon clad in a thousand lights and
armed against the night, beautiful though bold, brave
though shedding copious tears)
who showed her beautiful brow
crowned with morning glow, tender
and yet spirited prelude to the blazing
planet recruiting novice glimmerings as
troops, reserving more robust veteran lights

45 The sun.
46 Aurora, the dawn.

for the rearguard against the
tyrannous usurper[47] of
the empire of day, girdled in black laurel
of a thousand shadows made,
and with a fearsome nocturnal scepter she
governed the shadows that frightened even her.
But barely had the fair precursor, standard-
bearer to the Sun, raised her banner in the
orient than sweet yet martial clarions
of the birds sounded the call to arms (deft but
artless resounding trumpets),
when (like a cowardly tyrant, and hampered
by fearsome misgivings she tried to display
her forces, opposing brief repairs of her
gloomy cloak to the slashes
of light she received as wounds, though her courage
badly satisfied, was an ill-formed pretext
for her fear, knowing her resistance was weak),
trusting in flight more than force
to save her, she sounded her raucous cornet
to gather in the black squadrons and retreat
in order, just as she was attacked by a
nearer plenitude of gleamings that dawned on
the highest peak of the ramparts of the world.
The Sun, in short, arrived, closing the golden

47 Night. This passage describes the battle between night and day.

ring it engraved on a sapphire blue heaven:[48]
a thousand times thousand points,
a thousand golden flows (lines,
I say, of brilliant light) shone
from a luminous circumference, scoring
the cerulean page of the heavens, and
forming troops they charged the erstwhile ebony
tyrant of their empire, who in disorder hastily fled
stumbling on her own horrors,
treading on her own shadow,
attempting to reach the occident with her
now routed, disordered army of shadows,
pursued by the light following close behind.
At last her fugitive step came within view
of the occident, and (recovered from her
defeat, regaining her valor in ruins),
in the half of the world undefended by
the Sun, the second time a
rebel, determines to be crowned once again,
while the fair golden mane of the Sun lit our
hemisphere, with just light and distributive
order, gave all things visible their colors,
restoring to the external senses their
function, the world illuminated with more
certain light, and I, awake.

48 An allusion to the alternation of darkness and light on opposite sides of the
world.

PROLOGUE TO THE MYSTERY PLAY

DIVINE NARCISSUS

An Allegory

Occident

America

Zeal

Religion

Music

Soldiers

Scene I

(Enter OCCIDENT, an elegant Indian wearing a crown, and AMERICA at his side, an Indian noblewoman in the richly embroidered cloth and headdress worn when singing the tocotín.[1] *They sit on two chairs; around them dance Indian men and women, holding the feathers and shells ordinarily used in this dance; as they dance, MUSIC sings.)*

Music

Mexicans most noble,

whose ancient lineage

has its genesis in

the bright rays of the sun:

this is the blessed day,

---

1 An Aztec dance with its accompanying music.

the day in all the year
when we pay homage to
our highest deity;
then come now, come adorned
with your emblems of rank,
join to your piety
your joy, let them be one;
in festive pageantry
come worship and revere the great God of Seeds!

And since prosperity
in all our provinces
is owed to him who brings
abundance, pious ones,
make offerings to him
for they are owed to him
of the first fruits, bounty
of the year's rich harvest.
Let the finest blood flow
from your veins, blend the blood,
so it may serve his cult;
in festive pageantry
come worship and revere the great God of Seeds!

*(OCCIDENT and AMERICA take their seats, and
MUSIC falls silent.)*

Occident

> For among all the most high gods
> solemnly adored in my rites,
> so many deities that in
> this famed, illustrious city
> they number more than two thousand,
> to him we offer in savage
> unrelenting sacrifice hot
> human blood spilled, entrails throbbing,
> heart pulsating still, oh most cruel;
> and though they number so many
> (I say this again) my greatest
> devotion is fixed upon him,
> the highest of all the high gods,
> exalted, the great God of Seeds.

America

> And with reason, for this great god
> alone upholds our beloved
> realm, supporting our monarchy,
> sustaining our kingdom with his
> lush abundance of succulent
> fruits; this benefit is supreme,
> containing all other boons, since
> it preserves the life that it makes
> possible, and for this alone
> we deem it most precious of gifts;

knowing this truth, why would we care
that our mines, a bounty of gold,
make rich America richer,
if the miasma from those mines
turns fields barren, the fertile land
sown with seeds that once bloomed into
fruit, made desolate, a wasteland?
Then too, his divine protection
provides more than corporeal
food for us to eat. Afterward,
in precious viands sanctified,
formed from his own flesh (but purged first
of all bodily corruption)
he cleanses our souls of their stains.
And so, devoted to his cult,
let all of you repeat with me:

Occident, America, and Music
    In festive pageantry,
    come worship and revere the great God of Seeds!

Scene II

(They exit, dancing; enter the Christian RELIGION,[2]
a Spanish lady, and ZEAL,[3] an armed captain general,
and behind them, Spanish SOLDIERS.)

Religion

> You are Zeal, and being Zeal, how
> can your Christian fury bear to
> see idolatry, false and blind,
> celebrate with superstitious
> cults an idol, a vile affront
> to me, the Christian Religion?

Zeal

> Religion: please do not complain
> so quickly of my omission,
> or lament my poor blandishments;
> for my right arm now is upraised
> and brandishing my sword, and I
> shall avenge these wrongs, for your sake.
> Withdraw, my lady, to one side
> while I claim your rightful vengeance.

2 Religion represents the missionaries.
3 Zeal represents the conquistadors.

*(Enter OCCIDENT and AMERICA, dancing, and
from the other side MUSIC and accompaniment.)*

Music

In festive pageantry
come worship and revere the great God of Seeds!

Zeal

They have come out; I shall approach.

Religion

I shall go too; pity moves me
to draw near (before your anger
charges them, enraged, for my sake)
and invite them, in peace and love,
to receive the truth of my cult.

Zeal

Then let us hurry, for now they
have begun their indecent rite.

Music

In festive pageantry
come worship and revere the great God of Seeds!

(ZEAL and RELIGION approach.)

Religion

> Oh, most powerful Occident,
> beautiful, rich America,
> who live impoverished amid
> these prodigal bounties of wealth:
> put aside this blasphemous cult
> incited by Satan himself.
> Open your eyes! And now follow
> my true belief, the one true faith,
> persuaded by my Christian love.

Occident

> Who are they, what strangers are these
> I see before me? Oh heavens,
> why do they wish to impede the
> course of my joys and happiness?

America

> What nations unheard of and strange
> wish to counter the primacy
> of my most ancient rule and sway?

Occident

> Oh you, strange and foreign beauty,
> oh you, a lovely rare pilgrim!
> Tell me who you are who comes now
> to trouble my great jubilance.

Religion

> I am the Christian Religion,
> and I shall endeavor to turn
> your provinces to my worship.

Occident

> A fine avowal you demand!

America

> A fine lunacy you intend!

Occident

> What you contrive, impossible!

America

> No doubt she is mad; just leave her,
> and let our worship continue!

Occident, America, and Music

> And in festive pageantry,
> come worship and revere the great God of Seeds!

Zeal

> How, most barbarous Occident,
> and how, most blind idolatry,
> can you disdain sweet Religion,
> my dearly loved and gentle wife?

For you have already drained dry
the cup of your iniquities,
and our Lord God will not allow
you to continue your sinning,
and has sent me to punish you.

Occident

Who are you? The mere sight of your
face can strike fear deep in my heart.

Zeal

I am Zeal. Why are you surprised?
When all your excesses rebuff
Religion, my beloved spouse,
Zeal will appear to avenge her
by chastising your insolence.
A Minister of God am I,
and seeing that your tyrannies
have already gone so far, and
weary of seeing you live for
so many years in deep error,
He has sent me to punish you.
And therefore these mighty armed hosts,
vibrating thunderbolts of steel,
the ministers are of His wrath
and the instruments of His ire.

Occident

      What God, what error, what offense,

      what punishment do you proclaim?

      I do not understand your words,

      have no idea of your meaning,

      or who you are that you dare to

      interfere with the great task of

      my people as they gather here

      to recite as our cult demands:

Music

      And in festive pageantry,

      come worship and revere the great God of Seeds!

America

      Barbarian, madman, blindly

      with words none understands you wish

      to perturb the serenity

      that we enjoy in tranquil calm

      and peace: and cease in your efforts

      or you will be reduced to ash,

      and not even the winds will bear

      news that you once lived! And you, spouse,

      (To OCCIDENT.)

      and your vassals, be deaf and blind

to his words, ignore, do not heed
his fantasies; proceed with your
righteous worship, do not allow
upstart foreign nations in their
insolence to interrupt you.

Music

And in festive pageantry
come worship and revere the great God of Seeds!

Zeal

Since the first proposal of peace
you have so haughtily turned down,
then the second, for war, you must
accept despite your arrogance.
Sound the call! To arms! This is war!

(Drums and bugles sound.)

Occident

What monstrosities has heaven sent
against me? What weapons are these,
such arms my eyes have never seen?
Ah, my guards! And you, my soldiers:
those arrows you always prepare,
now is the time to let them fly!

America

    What lightning bolts does heaven hurl
    against me? What terrible orbs
    of burning lead rain down like hail?
    What monsters, hideous centaurs
    do battle against my people?

(Offstage voices)
    To arms, to arms! A war, a war!

(Instruments play)
    Long live Spain! And long live her king!

*(The battle is joined, the INDIANS enter through one
door and go out the other, the SPANIARDS in pursuit;
behind them, OCCIDENT retreats before RELI-
GION, and AMERICA before ZEAL.)*

SCENE III

Religion
    Surrender, haughty Occident!

Occident

> Now your valor must conquer me
> for I stand firm against mere words.

Zeal

> Die, insolent America!

Religion

> Wait, Zeal, wait, oh do not kill her,
> for I need her to be alive!

Zeal

> But how is it you defend her
> when you are the one offended?

Religion

> There can be no doubt: her conquest
> fell to your valor, your prowess,
> but what falls to me is mercy
> and the pity to spare her life;
> your charge, to conquer her by force,
> but mine to vanquish her with words,
> with the persuasive gentleness
> of mild, invincible reason.

Zeal

> You have seen the perversity
> in their blind abomination
> of your faith; is it not better
> that all die?

Religion

> Oh cease your justice,
> Zeal: you must not, cannot kill them:
> for I am by nature benign
> and I do not want them to die
> but to convert, and then to live.

America

> If your request that I not die
> and this show of your compassion
> are because, oh arrogant one,
> you expect to conquer me first
> with bodily weapons and then
> with the arms of intellect, you
> are mistaken, you are deceived;
> for although I, a captive, weep
> for my liberty, my free will
> with even greater liberty
> still will worship my deities!

Occident

> I have already said that force
> obliges me to cede to you;
> this is true, but hear me: clearly
> there is no force, no violence
> that can hinder my will, keep it
> from acting with total freedom;
> and so, as your captive I moan,
> but you cannot stop me, here, deep
> in my heart, from proclaiming that
> I worship and revere the great God of Seeds!

SCENE IV

Religion

> But wait, what I tender to you
> is not force but a mild caress.
> Which God is the one you revere?

Occident

> He is a God who makes fertile
> the fields that produce our harvests;
> before whom the heavens bow down,
> and whom even the rains obey;
> the same God who washes away

our sins, no matter how vile, then
becomes the food he offers us.
Tell me if there can ever be
from the most loving deity
more benefits for humankind
than these I describe for you now.

Religion (aside)

Lord save me! What crafty designs
and devices, what mimicries
do these falsehoods intend toward our
holiest, our most sacred truths?
Oh wiliest of serpents, most
venomous of snakes! Oh hydra[4]
spewing out of your seven mouths
all the deadly hemlock of that
most noxious poison, lethal brew!
How far will this malice of yours
imitate and feign the holy
miracles of our one true God?
But with your own lies and deceit,
if God grants this skill to my tongue,
I shall most surely convince you.

---

4 Hydra, snake, and serpent all refer to Satan.

America

> Oh, silent one, what is it you
> envision? Do you not see? No
> other God can confirm his works
> and his wonders with benefits.

Religion

> I must reason with the doctrine
> of Paul, for when he preached to the
> people of Athens he knew of
> their law that mandated death for
> any seeking to introduce
> new gods to the city; he was
> aware as well of the altar
> dedicated "to an unknown
> God," and declared these words to them:
> "This is not a new deity,
> no, this God I tell you about
> is the unknown God you worship
> and adore here at this altar."[5]
> I shall do the same . . . Occident,
> listen; blind idolatry, hear;
> for all your good fortune lies in
> heeding my words! Listen and hear.

5 Acts, 17:22–23.

Those miracles you tell about,
those prodigies you have revealed,
those glimmers and rare features glimpsed
behind the veils of false belief,
the curtains of superstition;
those portents that you misconstrue,
attributing wondrous effects,
to your gods of mendacity,
are works of the only true God
and of His infinite wisdom.
For if the flowering meadow
is fertile, if fields are fruitful,
and if the fruit proliferates,
and if the sown fields grow and bloom,
and if the clouds distill the rain,
all is the work of His right hand;
neither the arm that cultivates,
nor the rain that fecundates,
nor the warmth that animates, none
of these could make the plants flourish
and grow without the presence of
His productive Providence that
gives the plants their vegetative
soul.

America

   If all that you say is true,
  tell me: is this deity so
  benign that he will allow me
  to touch him with my own hands like
  the idol that my hands create,
  using the seeds and the rivers
  of innocent blood that is shed here,
  spilled here, caught for this one cause here,
  and for this sole effect alone?

Religion

  Even though His essence divine
  is invisible and immense,
  it is already deeply joined
  to our mundane, earthly nature,
  and draws near us so humanly
  that it allows the unworthy
  hands of priests, but no others, to
  approach the godhead and touch it.[6]

America

  In this, then, you and I agree,
  because as for my God, no one
  at all is sanctioned or allowed

---

6 This speech of Religion refers to the Incarnation and the Eucharist.

to touch him save those who serve him
as priests; and not only may they
not touch him, but the common folk,
the laity, may not even
enter his sanctified chapel.

Zeal

Oh what reverence, more worthy
to be paid to our one true God!

Occident

Tell me this, although you tell me
other things too: is this God made
of matter as fine and as rare
as the red blood shed and offered
in sacrifice, as the seed that
is our sustenance and support?

Religion

I said this before: His divine
majesty is infinite, not
material; but His blessed
humanity, bloodless in the
holy sacrifice of the Mass,
makes chance use of pure white wheat seeds
that then are transformed into His
very flesh, His very blood;

and His most precious blood, when caught
in the chalice, is the blood, pure
and innocent and pristine that,
offered on the altar of the
Holy Cross, is the salvation
and the redemption of the world.

America

Since you wish me to believe these
things that are unheard-of and strange,
can the deity you describe
be as loving as our God, the
one whom I adore, and offer
Himself to us as sustenance?

Religion

Yes, and all His divine wisdom,
for that aim and purpose alone,
dwells on earth among humankind.

America

And shall my eyes not see this God,
so that I may be persuaded,

Occident

and so that finally, at last,
my obstinacy will leave me?

Religion

> Yes, you will see when you are washed
> in the clear, crystalline fountain
> of Baptism.

Occident

> Oh yes, I know
> that before I sit at the rich
> table I must carefully wash,
> for that is my ancient custom.

Zeal

> That is not the kind of washing
> demanded by the stains you bear.

Occident

> What kind is it?

Religion

> A sacrament
> that like the living waters can
> wash away and cleanse all your sins.

America

> The brevity of the great news
> you bring confounds me, and I would
> like to hear this in detail once

more, for divine inspiration
moves me to want to fathom it.

Occident

And me; and to know of the life
and death of that resplendent God
who, you tell us, is in the bread.

Religion

All right, let us begin. First you
must know it is a metaphor,
an idea dressed in the colors
of rhetoric and visible
therefore to your eyes, as I shall
reveal to you; for I well know
you are more inclined to favor
objects that can be seen over
the words that faith can tell you;
and so, my friends, instead of ears
you need to use your eyes to learn
the teaching that faith will show you.

Occident

True: I would rather see it
than have you recount it to me.

SCENE V

Religion

    Let us begin.

Zeal

               Religion, please
tell me how you determine the
form to represent mysteries.

Religion

    In an allegorical play
I wish to make them visible
so that she and the entire
occident will be instructed
in all that they have desired
to know.

Zeal

               And what will you call the
play that you allegorize here?

Religion

    Divine Narcissus, because if
that most unhappy one had

an idol she truly worshipped,
whose strange signs and traits the Demon
attempted to twist into a
feigned high mystery of our faith
—the Holy Eucharist—know too
that there have been among other
Gentile peoples other signs and
traces of so high a marvel.

Zeal

And where will your play be performed?

Religion

In the crowned city of Madrid,
the royal center of our faith,
and the most regal seat and throne
of their Catholic Majesties
to whom the Indies owe the holy
lights of our most Christian Scripture
shining bright in the occident.

Zeal

Do you see impropriety
in writing it in Mexico
and performing it in Madrid?

Religion

> Do you mean you have never seen
> a thing created in one place
> that is of use in another?
> Moreover, writing it was not
> only a whim or mere caprice
> but an act of due obedience
> striving for the impossible.
> And so the work, perhaps rustic
> and rough, perhaps needing polish,
> is the result of obedience,
> not the child of audacity.

Zeal

> Well then, tell me, Religion, now
> that you have brought forth this play, how
> do you avoid the complaint
> that you introduce the Indies,
> then wish to take them to Madrid?

Religion

> Since the play intends only to
> celebrate this high mystery,
> and those who have been introduced
> are simply no more than a few
> abstractions that embody and

make visible what the play means,
nothing must be denied or changed
although I take them to Madrid:
for concepts of the intellect
no distances are a hindrance
and no oceans an obstacle.

Zeal

This being so, let us kneel before
the royal feet where two worlds meet
and most humbly beg for pardon;

Religion

and their bright, illustrious queen,

America

whose majestic, sovereign feet
the Indies do most humbly kiss;

Zeal

and her supreme noble councils;

Religion

her ladies who illuminate
their hemisphere;

America
                    and her wise men,
      whom my poor wisdom humbly prays
      to pardon and forgive its wish
      to summon a great mystery
      with these rough and clumsy verses.

Occident
      Let us begin, for my longing
      aches to see what the God is like
      who will be served to me as food,

      (AMERICA, OCCIDENT, and ZEAL all sing.)
      saying that only now
      do the Indies perceive
      who the true God of Seeds
      really is! And so we
      say that with tender tears
      distilled by our great joy,
      let all gaily repeat
      and raise rejoicing voices:

All

      Oh let us bless the day
      when we came to know the great true God of Seeds!

      (Exit dancing and singing.)

A LETTER

FROM SOR FILOTEA[1]
TO SOR JUANA INÉS DE LA CRUZ

---

1 The actual author was the Bishop of Puebla, don Manuel Fernández de
Santa Cruz.

Señora:

I have seen the letter from Your Grace in which you challenge the qualities of Christ which Reverend Father Antonio de Vieira described in his Maundy Thursday Sermon with so much subtlety that it has seemed to the most erudite men that, like another Eagle of the Apocalypse, this singular talent had soared beyond itself, following in the footsteps of the most Eminent César Meneses, one of the finest minds in Portugal; but in my judgment, whoever reads Your Grace's apologia cannot deny that your pen was cut finer than either of theirs, and they can take pride in finding themselves challenged by a woman who is the glory of her sex.

I, at least, have admired the acuteness of your concepts, the sagacity of your proofs, and the forceful clarity, inseparable companion of learning, with which you argue the matter, for the first word the Deity said was *light*, because without clarity there is no word for learning. Even Christ, when He spoke of the highest mysteries behind the veil of parables, was not admired in the world; only when He spoke clearly was He acclaimed for knowing everything.

This is one of the many benefits Your Grace owes to God, because clarity is not acquired through effort and industry: it is a gift that is infused with the soul.

I have had your letter printed so that Your Grace may be seen in better form and may recognize the treasures God has placed in your soul and, having more understanding, may be more grateful: for gratitude and understanding were always born at the same time. And if, as Your Grace says in your letter, whoever has received more from God has a greater obligation to repay, I fear Your Grace may be deeply in debt, for few creatures owe the Lord greater natural talents; therefore express your gratitude so that if until now you have used those talents well (which I believe of anyone who has entered your order), from now on you will use them better.

My judgment is not so austere a censor that it takes exception to your verses—for which Your Grace has been so celebrated—since Saint Teresa and Gregory of Nazianzus and other saints canonized this ability with their poems, but I should like you to imitate them in the choice of subjects as well as in technique.

I do not condone the vulgarity of those who reprove the practice of letters in women, for many applied themselves to this study, and not without the praise of Saint Jerome. True, Saint Paul says that women should not teach, but he does not direct women not to study in order to learn, because he wished only to avoid the danger of presumption in our sex, always so inclined to vanity. Divine Wisdom removed a letter from the name Sarai and added one to the name Abram, not because the man has to have more letters than the woman, as many believe, but because "i" added to the name Sara indicated pride and authority. *My lady* is translated as *Sarai*, and it was not proper for one who worked as a servant in the house of Abraham to be a lady.

God does not want letters that give rise to presumption in woman, but the Apostle does not censure letters unless they remove woman from a state of obedience. It is well known that study and learning have kept Your Grace in a subordinate state and helped you perfect the graces of obedience; for if other religious women sacrifice their will to obedience, Your Grace has ceded your understanding, which is the most arduous and pleasing offering that can be made in the name of a religious calling.

By giving this advice, it is not my intention that Your Grace alter your nature by renouncing books but improve it by reading the book of Jesus Christ from time to time. None of the Evangelists called the genealogy of Christ a book except Saint Matthew, because in his conversion he wished not to change his inclinations but to improve them, so that if once, as a tax collector, he spent his time on books that dealt with contracts and interest, as an Apostle he devoted himself to improving his nature by exchanging the books of his perdition for the book of Jesus Christ. Your Grace has spent a good deal of time studying philosophers and poets; now is the proper moment for you to perfect your pursuits and improve the books you read.

Was there ever a nation more erudite than Egypt? The first letters in the world originated there, and their hieroglyphics were a cause for astonishment. Extolling the wisdom of Joseph, Holy Scripture calls him unmatched in his knowledge of Egyptian erudition. And yet the Holy Spirit states openly that the Egyptian nation is barbaric, for all their learning merely penetrated the movements of the stars and the heavens but could not rein in the disorder of their passions; all their knowledge was devoted to perfecting man in his political life but did not enlighten him on how to attain the life eternal. And knowledge that does not light the way to salvation is deemed foolishness by God, Who knows all things.

This was the opinion of Justus Lipsius (a wonder of erudition) when he was close to death and the final reckoning, a time when our understanding is most enlightened: as his friends consoled him, recalling the many erudite books he had written, he said, pointing to a crucifix: *Knowledge that does not come from the Crucified God is foolishness and mere vanity.*

I do not condemn the reading of these authors for this reason, but I repeat to Your Grace what Gerson advised: Lend yourself to these studies, do not let them betray you or rob you. Human letters are slaves to divine letters and tend to make use of them, but should be condemned when they steal from Divine Widsom its possession of human understanding and transform those destined for servitude into fine ladies. They are commendable when the reason for curiosity, which is a vice, becomes studiousness, which is a virtue.

The angels whipped Saint Jerome because he read Cicero, seduced rather than as a free man, as he preferred the delight of his eloquence to the solidity of Holy Scripture; yet it is to be commended that the Holy Doctor made use of the facts and profane erudition obtained from such authors.

The time Your Grace has spent on fields of knowledge that arouse curiosity is not negligible; now, like the great Boethius, turn your attention to fields that are more profitable, joining to the subtleties of natural knowledge the usefulness of moral philosophy.

It is a pity when so great an understanding becomes so immersed in base earthly matters that it does not wish to penetrate what occurs in Heaven; and since you humble yourself to the earth, sink no lower but consider what happens in Hell. And if on occasion you desire sweet and tender tidings, turn your understanding to Mount Calvary, where, observing the loving kindness of the Redeemer and the ingratitude of the redeemed, you will find ample scope for pondering the abundance of infinite love and marshaling a defense, not without tears, against utmost ingratitude. Or, on other occasions, most usefully launch the magnificent galleon of Your Grace's intelligence onto the high seas of divine perfections. I have no doubt that you will have the same experience as Apelles, who painted the portrait of Campaspe, and with each stroke of his brush on the canvas, the arrow of love left a wound in his heart, so that the painter was at once perfecting the portrait while his love for the original inflicted mortal wounds to his heart.

I am very certain that if Your Grace, with the keen rationality of your understanding, were to form and depict an idea of divine perfections (whatever the dark shadows of faith allow), at the same time you would find your soul illuminated by light and your will blazing with and sweetly wounded by love of God, so that Our Lord, who has so abundantly showered Your Grace's nature with positive benefits, will not find Himself obliged to grant only negative benefits to your spirit; for no matter how Your Grace's intelligence may call them kindnesses, I deem them punishments, because it is a benefit only when God prepares the human heart with His Grace so that we may respond with gratitude, making use of a recognized benefit so that Divine Generosity is not held back but makes those benefits even greater.

This is the wish for Your Grace of one who, ever since she kissed your hand many years ago, has lived enamored of your soul with a love that neither distance nor time has cooled; for spiritual love does not suffer periods of mutability, and love that is pure does not acknowledge mutability unless it leads to growth. May Our Lord hear my prayers and make Your Grace very holy and keep you well.

From the Convent of the Holy Trinity, in Puebla de los Ángeles, 25 November 1690.

I kiss Your Grace's hand and am your affectionate servant,

Filotea de la Cruz

RESPONSE *of the* POET

TO THE VERY EMINENT
SOR FILOTEA DE LA CRUZ

Very eminent lady, my señora:

Neither my will nor scant health nor reasonable apprehension has delayed my response for so many days. Is it any surprise that my dull pen stumbled over two impossibilities at its first step? The first (and for me the more severe) is how to respond to your most learned, most prudent, most saintly, and most loving letter. For if the Angelic Doctor of the Schools, Saint Thomas, when questioned regarding his silence in the presence of Albertus Magnus, his teacher, replied that he was silent because he could find nothing to say worthy of Albertus, with how much more reason should I be silent, not, like the saint, out of humility, but because in reality, I know nothing worthy of you. The second impossibility is how to thank you for the favor, as unwarranted as it was unexpected, of having my rough scribblings printed; a good turn so immeasurable that it surpasses the most ambitious hope and most fantastic desire, which could find no place, even as a rational concept, in my thoughts; in short, it is of such magnitude that it not only cannot be reduced to the limits of words but exceeds the capacity of gratitude, as much for its dimensions as for how unforeseen it was, for as

Quintilian said: *Hopes give rise to the lesser glory, benefits to the greater.* So much so that they silence the beneficiary.

When the happily barren, only to be made miraculously fruitful, mother of the Baptist saw so magnificent a visitor as the Mother of the Word in her house, her understanding became clouded and her speech failed, and so instead of thanks she burst into doubts and questions: *Et unde hoc mihi?* From whence comes such a thing to me? The same occurred to Saul when he found himself elected and anointed king of Israel: *Am I not a son of Jemini of the least tribe of Israel, and my kindred the last among all the families of the tribe of Benjamin? Wherefore then hast thou spoken this word to me?*[1] And so say I: from whence, illustrious señora, from whence comes so great a favor to me? Am I by chance anything more than a poor nun, the most insignificant creature in the world and the least worthy of your attention? *Wherefore then speakest thou so to me? From whence comes such a thing to me?*

To the first impossibility I can respond only that I am unworthy of your eyes, and to the second I cannot respond with anything other than exclamations, not thanks, saying that I am not capable of offering you even the smallest portion of the gratitude I owe you. It is not false modesty, señora, but the candid truth of all my soul, that when the letter your eminence

---

1 1 Samuel 9:21 (from the Douay-Rheims English version of the Latin Vulgate Bible, translated by St. Jerome and cited by Sor Juana; abbreviated as D-R). All other biblical citations in this letter refer to the King James Version.

called *Atenagórica*[2] reached me, I burst (although this does not come easily to me) into tears of confusion, because it seemed that your favor was nothing more than a reproach from God for how poorly I meet His expectations; while He corrects others with punishments, He wants to reduce me by means of benefits. A special favor, for which I know I am in His debt, as I am for other infinite benefits from His immense kindness, but also a special mode of shaming and confusing me: for it is a more exquisite method of punishment to have me, with my knowledge, serve as the judge who sentences and condemns my own ingratitude. When I ponder this, here in solitude, I often say: Lord may You be blessed, for You not only did not wish any other creature to judge me, and did not give me that responsibility either, but kept it for Yourself and freed me from me and the sentence I would have given myself—which, compelled by my own knowledge, could not be less than condemnation— and reserved that for Your mercy, because You love me more that I can love myself.

Señora, forgive the digression that the power of truth demanded of me, and if I must confess the whole truth, this is also a search for havens to escape the difficulty of responding, and I almost decided to leave everything in silence, but since this is negative, although it explains a great deal with the emphasis on not explaining, it is necessary to add a brief explanation so that what one wishes the silence to say is

2 It is assumed that "worthy of Athena" is the translation.

understood; if not, the silence will say nothing, because that is its proper occupation: saying nothing. The sacred chosen vessel was carried away to the third heaven, and having seen the arcane secrets of God, the text says: *He . . . heard secret words, which it is not granted to man to utter.*[3] It does not say what he saw but says that he cannot say; and so it is necessary at least to say that those things that cannot be said cannot be said, so it is understood that being silent does not mean having nothing to say, but that the great deal there is to say cannot be said in words. Saint John says that if all the miracles performed by Our Redeemer were to be written down, the entire world could not hold the books; and Vieira states that the Evangelist says more in just this passage than in everything else he wrote; the Lusitanian Phoenix speaks very well (but when does he not speak well, even when he does not speak well?), because here Saint John says everything he did not say and expressed what he did not express. And I, señora, will respond only that I do not know how to respond, will only give thanks, saying I am not capable of giving thanks to you, and will say, as a brief explanation of what I leave to silence, that only with the confidence of a favored woman and the benefits of an honored one can I dare speak to your excellency. If this is foolishness, forgive it, for it is a jewel of good fortune, and in it I will provide more material for your kindness, and you will give greater form to my gratitude.

3 2 Corinthians 12:4 (D-R).

Because he stammered, Moses did not think he was worthy to speak to the Pharaoh, and afterward, finding himself so favored by God fills him with so much courage that he not only speaks to God Himself but dares ask Him for impossibilities: *Shew me thy face.*[4] And I too, señora, no longer think impossible what I wrote at the beginning, in view of how you favor me; because the person who had the letter printed without my knowledge, who gave it a title and paid for it, who honored it so greatly (since it is entirely unworthy both for its own sake and the sake of its author), what will she not do, what will she not pardon, what will she cease doing, and what will she cease pardoning? And so, under the assumption that I speak with the safe-conduct of your favors and under the protection of your kindness, and your having, like another Ahasuerus, given me the tip of the golden scepter of your affection to kiss as a sign of granting me benevolent license to speak[5] and propound in your illustrious presence, I say that I receive in my soul your most saintly admonition to turn my studies to sacred books, which although this comes in the guise of advice will have for me the substance of a precept, with the not insignificant consolation that even earlier it seems my obedience foresaw your pastoral suggestion, as well as your guidance, inferred from the subject and proofs of the same letter. I know very well that your most

4 Exodus 33:13 (D-R).
5 This is how Ahasuerus gave Esther permission to speak, in Esther 5:2.

sage warning is not directed at it but at how much you have seen of my writings on human affairs; and so what I have said is only to satisfy you with regard to the lack of application you have inferred (and rightly so) from other writings of mine. And speaking more specifically I confess, with the candor that is owed you and with the truth and clarity that in me are always natural and customary, that my not having written a great deal about sacred matters has been due not to defiance or lack of application but to an abundance of the fear and reverence owed to those sacred letters, for whose comprehension I know myself highly incapable and for whose handling I am highly unworthy; resounding always in my ears, with no small horror, is the Lord's warning and prohibition to sinners like me: *Why dost thou declare my justices, and take my covenant in thy mouth?*[6] My great father Saint Jerome confirms this question, and that even learned men are forbidden to read the Song of Solomon and even Genesis before the age of thirty (the latter because of its obscurity, the former so that imprudent youth will not use the sweetness of those nuptial songs as an excuse to alter their meaning to carnal love), by ordering that it be the last book studied, for the same reason: *At the end one may read, without danger, the Song of Songs; for if it is read at the beginning, when one does not understand the epithalamium to the spiritual marriage beneath*

6 Psalm 49:16 (D-R).

the carnal words, one may suffer harm;[7] and Seneca says: *In the early years, faith is not bright.*[8] Then how would I dare hold it in my unworthy hands, when it is in conflict with my sex, my age, and especially, my customs? And so I confess that often this fear has removed the pen from my hand and made subjects withdraw into the same understanding from which they wished to emerge; this difficulty was not encountered in profane subjects, for a heresy against art is punished not by the Holy Office but by the prudent with laughter and the critics with condemnation; and this, just or unjust, there is no reason to fear it, for one can still take Communion and hear Mass and therefore it concerns me very little or not at all; because according to the same opinion of those who cast aspersions, I have no obligation to know and no aptitude for being correct; therefore, if I err there is no blame and no discredit. There is no blame because I have no obligation; there is no discredit because I have no possibility of being correct, and no one is obliged to undertake impossible things. And, truly, I have never written except reluctantly, when I was forced to, and only to please others; not only with no gratification but with positive repugnance, for I have never judged myself to possess the abundance of letters and intelligence demanded by the obligation of one who writes; and so my usual reply to those who urge me to write, especially if the

7 St. Jerome, *To Leta, Upon the Education of Her Daughter* (written c. 403 CE).
8 Seneca, *De beneficiis.*

subject is sacred: "What understanding, what studies, what materials, what rudimentary knowledge do I possess for this other than some superficial nonsense? Leave this for someone who understands it, for I wish no quarrel with the Holy Office, for I am ignorant and terrified of stating an offensive proposition or twisting the genuine significance of some passage. I do not study to write, much less to teach (which would be excessive pride in me), but only to see whether by studying I will be less ignorant." This is how I respond and how I feel.

Writing has never been by my own volition but at the behest of others; for I could truthfully say to them: *Ye have compelled me.*[9] A truth I will not deny (one, because it is widely known, and two, because even if used against me, God has favored me with a great love of the truth) is that ever since the first light of reason struck me, my inclination toward letters has been so strong and powerful that neither the reprimands of others—I have had many—nor my own reflections—I have engaged in more than a few—have sufficed to make me abandon this natural impulse that God placed in me: His Majesty knows why and to what end; and He knows I have asked Him to dim the light of my understanding, leaving only enough for me to obey His Law, for anything else is too much in a woman, according to some; there are even those who say it does harm. Almighty God knows too that when I did not obtain this, I attempted to

9 2 Corinthians 12:11.

bury my understanding along with my name and sacrifice it to the One who gave it to me; for no other reason did I enter a convent, although the spiritual exercises and companionship of a community were incompatible with the freedom and quiet my studious intentions demanded; and afterward, in the community, the Lord knows, as does the only one in the world, that once in the community I attempted to hide my name but was not permitted to, for it was said it was a temptation; and it would have been. If I could pay you, señora, something of what I owe you, I believe I could only pay you in full by telling you this, for I have never spoken of it except to the one who had to hear it. But having opened wide the doors of my heart to you, revealing its deepest secrets, I want you to find my confidence worthy of what I owe to your illustrious person and excessive favors.

I

Continuing the narration of my inclination, about which I want to give you a complete account, I say that before I was three years old my mother sent an older sister of mine to learn to read in one of the primary schools for girls called *Friends*, and, led by affection and mischief, I followed after her; and seeing that she was being taught a lesson, I was so set ablaze by the desire to know how to read that in the belief I was deceiving her, I told the teacher my mother wanted her to give me a lesson too. She did not believe it, because it was not believable, but to go along with the joke, she taught me. I continued to go and she continued to teach me, in earnest now, because with experience she realized the truth; and I learned to read in so short a time that I already knew how when my mother found out, for the teacher hid it from her in order to give her complete gratification and receive her reward at the same time; and I kept silent believing I would be whipped for having done this without her knowledge. The woman who taught me is still alive (may God keep her), and she can testify to this.

I remember at this time, my appetite being what is usual at that age, I abstained from eating cheese because I had heard it made people stupid, and my desire to learn was stronger in me than the desire to eat, despite this being so powerful in children. Later, when I was six or seven years old and already knew how to read and write, along with all the other skills pertaining to sewing and needlework learned by women, I heard there was a university and schools in Mexico City where sciences were studied; as soon as I heard this I began to pester my mother with insistent, inopportune pleas that she send me, dressed as a boy, to the home of some relatives she had in Mexico City, so I could study and attend classes at the university; she refused, and rightly so, but I satisfied my desire by reading many different books owned by my grandfather, and there were not enough punishments and reprimands to stop me, so that when I came to Mexico City, people were surprised not so much by my intelligence as by my memory and the knowledge I possessed at an age when it seemed I had barely had enough time to learn to speak.

I began to learn Latin and believe I had fewer than twenty lessons; my seriousness was so intense that since the natural adornment of hair is so admired in women—especially in the flower of one's youth—I would cut off four to six inches, first measuring how long it was and then imposing on myself the rule that if, when it had grown back, I did not know whatever I had proposed to learn while it was growing, I would cut it again as a punishment for my stupidity. And when it grew back and I did not know what I had determined to learn, because my hair grew quickly and I learned slowly, then in fact I did cut it as punishment for my stupidity, for it did not seem right for my head to be dressed in hair when it was so bare of knowledge, which was a more desirable adornment. I entered the convent although I knew the situation had certain characteristics (I speak of secondary qualities, not formal ones) incompatible with my character, but considering the total antipathy I had toward matrimony, the convent was the least disproportionate and most honorable decision I could make to provide the certainty I desired for my salvation, and the first (and in the end the most important) obstacle to overcome was to relinquish all the minor defects in my character, such as wanting to live alone, and not wanting any obligatory occupation that would limit the freedom of my studies, or the noise of a community that would interfere with the tranquil silence of my books. These made me hesitate somewhat in my determination, until learned persons enlightened me, saying they were a temptation, which I overcame with Divine Grace and entered into the state I so unworthily am in now. I thought I would flee myself, but I, poor wretch, brought myself with me as well as this inclination, my greatest enemy (I cannot determine whether Heaven gave it to me as a gift or a punishment), for when it was dimmed or interfered with by the many spiritual exercises present in the religious life, it exploded in me like gunpowder, proof in my own person that privation is the cause of appetite.

I returned to (no, I am wrong, for I never stopped): I mean to say I continued my studious effort (which for me was repose whenever I had time away from my obligations) to read and read some more, to study and study some more, with no teacher other than the books themselves. I learned how difficult it is to study those soulless characters without the living voice and explanations of a teacher; yet I gladly endured all this work for the sake of my love of letters. Oh, if it had only been for the sake of my love of God, which is the correct love, how meritorious it would have been! I did attempt to elevate it as much as I could and turn it to His service, because the goal to which I aspired was the study of theology, for, being Catholic, it seemed a foolish lack in me not to know everything that can be learned in this life, by natural means, about the Divine Mysteries; and being a nun and not a layperson, according to my ecclesiastical state I should profess vows to letters, and even more so, as a daughter of a Saint Jerome and a Saint Paula, for it seemed a deterioration if such learned parents produced an idiot child. I proposed this to myself and it seemed correct, if it was not (and this is most likely) flattery and applause of my own inclination, its enjoyment being proposed as an obligation.

In this way I proceeded, always directing the steps of my study to the summit of sacred theology, as I have said; and to reach it, I thought it necessary to ascend by the steps of human sciences and arts, because how is one to understand the style of the queen of sciences without knowing that of the handmaidens? How, without logic, was I to know the general and particular methods used in the writing of Holy Scripture? How, without rhetoric, would I understand its figures, tropes, and locutions? How, without physics, comprehend the many inherent questions concerning the nature of the animals used for sacrifices, in which so many stated subjects, as well as many others that are undeclared, are symbolized? How to know whether Saul healing at the sound of David's harp came from the virtue and natural power of music or the supernatural ability God wished to place in David? How, without arithmetic, understand so many computations of years, days, months, hours, and weeks as mysterious as those in Daniel, and others for whose deciphering one must know the natures, concordances, and properties of numbers? How, without geometry, can one measure the Holy Ark of the Covenant and the holy city of Jerusalem, whose mysterious measurements form a cube with all its dimensions, a marvelous proportional distribution of all its parts? How, without architecture, fathom the great temple of Solomon, where God Himself was the artificer, conceiving the proportion and design, and the wise king merely the overseer who executed it; where there was no base without a mystery, no column without a symbol, no cornice without an allusion, no architrave without a meaning, and so on in all its parts, so that even the smallest fillet was placed not for the service and complement of art alone but to symbolize greater things? How, without great knowledge of the rules and parts that constitute history, can the historical books be understood? Those recapitulations in which what happened earlier often is placed later in the narration and seems to have occurred afterward? How, without great familiarity with both kinds of law, can one apprehend the legal books? How, without great erudition, approach so many matters of profane history mentioned in Holy Scripture, so many Gentile customs, so many rites, so many ways of speaking? How, without many rules and much reading of the Holy Fathers, can one grasp the obscure expression of the prophets? And without being very expert in music, how are we to understand the musical proportions and their beauty found in so many places, especially in the petition of Abraham to

God on behalf of the cities,[10] that He spare them if He found fifty righteous men, and from this number he went down to forty-five, which is a sesquinona [a minor whole tone or minor second], going from *mi* to *re*; and from here to forty, which is a sesquioctava [a major whole tone or major second], going from *re* to *ut* [modern *do*];[11] from here to thirty which is a sesquitertia, a diatessaron [a perfect fourth]; from here to twenty, which is the sesquialtera proportion, a diapente [a perfect fifth]; from here to ten, which is the dupla, a diapason [an octave]; and since there are no other harmonic intervals, he went no further? Well, how could one understand this without music? In the Book of Job, God says: *Shalt thou be able to join together the shining stars the Pleiades, or canst thou stop the turning about of Arcturus? Canst*

10 See Genesis 28:24–32.

11 Sor Juana apparently erred, or the text has been corrupted, when she indicated that the sesquioctava was from *re* to *mi*, the same illustration used for the sesquinona. This has been corrected to "from *re* to *ut*." The sesquinona and sesquioctava are two different types of the interval now known as a whole tone or second. There are no modern equivalents to these two kinds of whole tone. Our thanks to Professor Mario A. Ortiz, Catholic University of America, for his invaluable assistance in clarifying the musical terminology and the Pythagorean concepts presented in this section.

As indicated by Cecil Adkins, "Monochord," *Grove Music Online, Oxford Music Online*, Oxford University Press, accessed Otober 31, 2013, www.oxford musiconline.com/subscriber/article/grove/music/18973/, "The Pythagorean concept of division by proportions is based on the relationship of the harmonic and arithmetic means as they are represented by the numbers 6, 8, 9, and 12. The ratio 12:6 produces the octave; 9:6 and 12:8, the 5th; 8:6 and 12:9, the 4th; and 9:8, the major 2nd. Reduced to their lowest terms these ratios are dupla (12:1), sesquialtera (3:2), sesquitertia (4:3) and sesquioctava (9:8)."

thou bring forth the day star in its time and make the evening star to rise upon the children of the earth?[12] The terms, without knowledge of astronomy, would be impossible to comprehend. And not only these noble sciences, but there is no mechanical art that is not mentioned. In short, it is the book that encompasses all books, and the science that includes all sciences, which are useful for its understanding: even after learning all of them (which clearly is not easy, or even possible), another consideration demands more than all that has been said, and that is constant prayer and purity in one's life, in order to implore God for the purification of spirit and enlightenment of mind necessary for comprehending these lofty matters; if this is lacking, the rest is useless.

The Church says these words regarding the angelic doctor Saint Thomas: When he read the most difficult passages of Holy Scripture, he combined fasting with prayer. And he would say to his companion, Brother Reginald, that all he knew was not due to study or his own labor, but that he had received it from God.[13] And I, so distant from virtue and from letters, how was I to have the courage to write? Therefore, having attained a few elementary skills, I continually studied a variety of subjects, not having an inclination toward one in particular but toward all of them in general; as a consequence, having studied some more than

---

12 Job 38:31–32 (D-R).
13 Roman Breviary, Office of the Feast of St. Thomas [Aquinas], March 7, Fifth Lesson.

others has not been by choice but because, by chance, I had access to more books about those subjects, which created the preference more than any decision of mine. And since I had no special interest that moved me, and no time limit that restricted my continuing to study one subject because of the demands of formal classes, I could study a variety of subjects or abandon some for others, although I did observe a certain order, for some I called study and others diversion, and with these I rested from the first, with the result that I have studied many subjects and know nothing, because some have interfered with my learning others. True, I say this regarding the practical aspect of those subjects that have one, because it is obvious that while one moves a pen, the compass does nothing, and while one plays the harp, the organ is silent, and so on; because since a great deal of physical practice is necessary to acquire a practical skill, the person who is divided among various exercises can never achieve perfection; but the opposite happens in formal and speculative areas, and I would like to persuade everyone with my experience that this not only does not interfere but helps, for one subject illuminates and opens a path in another by means of variations and hidden connections—placed in this universal chain by the wisdom of its Author—so that it seems they correspond and are joined with admirable unity and harmony. It is the chain the ancients imagined issuing from the mouth of Jupiter, where all things hung linked to all other things. Reverend Father Athanasius

Kircher demonstrates this in his curious book *De Magnete*. All things emanate from God, Who is at once the center and circumference from which all created lines emerge and where they end.

As for me, I can state that what I do not understand in an author from one discipline I usually can understand in a different author from another discipline that seems quite distant from the first; and in their explanations, these authors offer metaphorical examples from other arts, as when logicians say that the mean is to the terms as a measurement is to two distant bodies, in order to determine whether they are equal; and that the statement of a logician moves, like a straight line, along the shortest path, while that of a rhetorician follows, like a curve, the longest, but both travel to the same point; and when it is said that expositors are like an open hand and scholastics like a closed fist. This is not an excuse for having studied a diversity of subjects, nor do I offer it as such, for these subjects contribute to one another, but my not having benefitted from them has been the fault of my ineptitude and the weakness in my understanding, not of their variety.

II

What might absolve me is the immense amount of work caused by lacking not only a teacher but other students with whom to confer and practice what I studied, having a mute book for a teacher and an insentient inkwell for a fellow student; and instead of explanation and practice, countless obstacles, not only those of my religious obligations (and we already know what a helpful and profitable use of time these are) but those other things that are inevitable in a community: for instance, when I am reading and in the adjoining cell they take a notion to play their instruments and sing; when I am studying and two maidservants have a quarrel and come to have me judge their dispute; when I am writing and a friend comes to visit, doing me a disservice with nothing but good intentions, and it is necessary not only to accept the intrusion but be grateful for the damage done. And this happens constantly, because since the times I devote to my studies are those not dedicated to the routine duties of the community, those same times are moments of leisure for the other sisters who interrupt me; and only those who have experienced communal life know how true this is, for only the strength of my vocation and the great love that exists among me and my beloved sisters can make my disposition agreeable, and since love is harmony, in it there are no polar opposites.

I do confess that my work has been interminable, which means I cannot say what I enviously hear others say: that they have not had to work for knowledge. How fortunate for them! For me, not the knowing (for I still know nothing) but only the desire to know has been so difficult that I could say with my father Saint Jerome (although not with his achievements): The labor it has cost me, the difficulties I have endured, the times I have despaired, and the other times I have desisted and begun again, all because of my determination to learn, to what I have suffered my conscience is witness and the conscience of those who have lived with me.[14] Except for the companions and witnesses (for I have lacked even that solace), I can affirm the truth of the rest. And that my unfortunate inclination has been so great it has overcome everything else!

It used to happen that since a kind, affable temperament is one of the many benefits I owe to God, the other nuns were very fond of me (without noticing, like the good women they are, my faults) and as a consequence they enjoyed my company; knowing this, and moved by the great love I had for them, with more reason than they had for loving me, I enjoyed their company even more; and so, during the times all of us had free, I would go to cheer them and take pleasure in their conversation. I noticed that during these times I lost the opportunity to study, and I vowed not to enter any cell unless obliged to by obedience or charity, because without this severe restraint, the deterrent of mere intention would be broken by my love; and this vow (knowing my weakness) I would make for a month or for two weeks; and when it was fulfilled I would renew it, giving myself a day or two of respite and using that time not so much for rest (for not

14 Letter from St. Jerome to Rusticus (a monk), 411 CE.

studying has never been restful to me) as for keeping my dearly loved sisters from thinking me harsh, withdrawn, and ungrateful for their undeserved affection.

It is clear from this how strong my inclination is. I thank God for willing that it be turned to letters and not another vice, for it was practically unconquerable; and it can easily be inferred how my poor studies have sailed against the current (or rather, how they have foundered). For I still have not recounted the most arduous of the difficulties; those I have described so far have been merely obligatory or accidental obstacles, and therefore indirect. I have not touched on the direct ones whose intent was to interfere with and prevent my studies. Who would not think, seeing the widespread acclaim I have received, that I sailed calm seas with the wind behind me, surrounded by the applause of general approbation? But God knows it has not been so, because among the flowers of these same acclamations more serpents than I can count of rivalries and persecutions have arisen and awakened, and the most noxious and hurtful to me have been not those who persecuted me with open hatred and malice but those who, loving me and desiring my welfare (and perhaps deserving a great deal from God for their good intentions), mortified and tormented me more than the others, saying: "Her studies are not in accord with holy ignorance; she will surely be lost, and at such heights her own perspicacity and wit are bound to make her vain." What did it cost me to endure this? A strange kind of martyrdom, in which I was both the martyr and my own executioner!

As for my ability—doubly unfortunate in me—to compose verses, even if religious, what sorrows has it not caused me, and causes me still? In truth, señora, at times I begin to think that the one who excels—or is made to excel by God, Who alone can effect this—is received as a common enemy, because it seems to some that this person usurps the applause they deserve or blocks the admiration to which they aspire, and so they persecute this person.

That politically barbarous law of Athens, by which whoever excelled in gifts and virtues was exiled from the republic to keep him from tyrannizing public liberty with those gifts, still endures and is still observed in our day, although the motive of the Athenians no longer exists; but there is another one, no less effective although not as well founded, for it seems a maxim of the impious Machiavelli, and that is to despise the one who excels because that person discredits others. This occurs, and has always occurred.

If this is not so, what caused the rabid hatred of the Pharisees toward Christ, when there were so many reasons for them to feel otherwise? For if we consider His presence, what gift was more worthy of love than His divine beauty? What gift more powerful in captivating hearts? If human comeliness rules our wills, and with tender and longed-for desired force knows how to subject them, what would be the effect of His beauty with its countless prerogatives and sovereign charms? What would that incomprehensible comeliness do, what would it move, what would it not do and not move, when from that beautiful face, as if from polished crystal, the beams of Divinity shone through? What could that countenance not move, when above and beyond incomparable human perfections, it also disclosed illuminations of the divine? If the face of Moses, after only conversing with God, proved unendurable to the fragility of human eyes,[15] what would the humanized face of God Himself be like? And if we turn to His other gifts, what more worthy of love than that celestial modesty, that gentleness and tenderness pouring forth mercy in all His movements, that profound humility and compassion, those words of eternal life and eternal wisdom? How is it possible that all of this did not stir their souls to follow Him, did not elevate them and fill them with love?

My holy mother Saint Teresa says that after she saw the beauty of Christ, she could never again feel an inclination toward any creature because she saw nothing that was not ugly compared to that beauty. How could it have had such contrary effects in men? And even if they were rough and base and had no knowledge of or esteem for His perfections, not even as possibly profitable, how could they not be moved by the advantage and usefulness of all the benefits received from Him: healing the sick, resuscitating the dead,

15 Exodus 34:29–30.

curing those possessed by the devil? How could they not love Him? Oh, God, that was precisely why they did not love Him, that was precisely why they despised Him! They themselves bore witness to that.

They met in their council and said: *What do we? For this man doeth many miracles.*[16] Can this be a motive? If they had said: "This man is a malefactor, a transgressor against the law, an agitator who with deceptions stirs up the people," they would have lied, as they lied when they did say these things; yet there were more coherent reasons for doing what they asked, which was to take His life, but to give as a reason that He performed miracles does not seem worthy of learned men, which the Pharisees were. And so it is that when learned men are overcome by passion, they spew forth these kinds of irrelevancies. Indeed, only for that reason was it determined that Christ should die. Men, if I can call you that when you are so brutish, what was the reason for so cruel a determination? Their only response is *multa signa facit.* Lord have mercy if doing excellent things is a reason to die! This *multa signa facit* evokes *there shall be a root of Jesse, which shall stand for an ensign of the people*[17] and then to *this child . . . [is] a sign which shall be spoken against.*[18]

16 John 11:47.
17 Isaiah 11:10.
18 Luke 2:34.

He is a sign? Then He must die! He excels? Then He must suffer, for that is the reward of one who excels!

Figures of the winds and of fame are usually placed at the very top of temples as decoration, and to protect them from birds, they are covered by barbs; this seems a protection yet is nothing but an inevitable attribute: whoever is on high is necessarily pierced by barbs. The animosity of the wind is there, the severity of the elements, the fury of thunderbolts taking their revenge, there is the target of stones and arrows. Oh unhappy heights, exposed to so many risks! Oh excellence, made a target of envy and the object of hostility! Any eminence, whether of dignity, nobility, wealth, beauty, or knowledge, suffers this burden, but the one that suffers most severely is understanding. First, because it is the most defenseless, since wealth and power punish any who attacks them, but not understanding, for the greater it is, the more modest and long-suffering and the less it defends itself. Second, because as Gracián so wisely said, the advantages of understanding are advantages in one's being. For no other reason than greater understanding are angels more than men; and men surpass brutes only in understanding; and since no one wants to be less than another, no man confesses that another understands more, because that is the consequence of being more. A man will suffer and confess that another is more noble than he, wealthier, handsomer, and even more learned; but there is hardly anyone who will confess that another has more understanding: rare is the man who will concede cleverness. That is why attacks against this gift are so effective.

When the soldiers mocked and jeered and taunted Our Lord Jesus Christ, they brought an old purple cloth and a hollow reed and a crown of thorns to crown Him a derisory king. Now, the reed and the purple cloth were insulting, but not painful; why was only the crown painful? Was it not enough that, like the other emblems, it would be mocking and ignominious, since that was its purpose? No, because the sacred head of Christ and His divine brain were the repository of wisdom; and it is not enough in the world for a wise brain to be ridiculed, it must also be wounded and mistreated; a head that is a treasury of wisdom should not expect any crown other than one of thorns. What garland can human wisdom expect when it sees what divine wisdom received? Roman pride also crowned the various feats of its captains with various crowns: the civic for the man who defended the city, the military for the man who penetrated the enemy camp, the mural for the man who scaled the wall, the obsidional for the man who freed a besieged city or army or field or camp, the naval, the oval, the triumphal for other deeds, as recounted by Pliny and Aulus Gellius; but considering so many different kinds of crowns, I wondered which type was used for the crown of Christ, and I think it was the obsidional, which (as you know, señora) was the most honorable and called obsidional from *obsidio*, which means "siege"; it was not made of gold or silver but of the very grain or grass growing in the field where the feat was accomplished. And since the feat of Christ was to raise the siege of the Prince of Darkness, who had besieged all the world, as it says in the Book of Job: *From going to and fro in the earth, and from walking up and down in it*;[19] and as Saint Peter says: *the devil . . . walketh about, seeking whom he may devour*;[20] and Our Lord came and raised the siege: *now shall the prince of this world be cast out*,[21] and so the soldiers crowned Him not with gold or silver but with the natural fruit produced by the world, which was the battlefield that, after the curse, *thorns also and thistles shall it bring forth to thee*,[22] produced nothing but thorns; therefore it was the most suitable crown for the valiant and wise Conqueror, crowned by His mother the Synagogue; and the daughters of Zion came out weeping to see His sorrowful triumph, as they had come rejoicing for the other Solomon, because the triumph of the wise is achieved with sorrow and celebrated with weeping, which is how wisdom triumphs; and since Christ, as the King of Wisdom, was the first to wear the crown that was made holy on His temples, other wise men are no longer afraid and understand they cannot aspire to any other honor.

19 Job 1:7.
20 1 Peter 5:8.
21 John 12:31.
22 Genesis 3:18.

Life Himself wished to give life to the deceased Lazarus; the Disciples were not aware of His intention and replied: *Master, the Jews of late sought to stone thee; and goest thou thither again?* The Redeemer assuaged their fear: *Are there not twelve hours in the day?*[23] Up to this point it seems they were afraid because of the antecedent of the people wanting to stone Him when He reproached them, calling them thieves and not shepherds. And so they feared that if He returned to the same place (since no matter how just, rebukes are not often acknowledged as true), He would put His life in danger; but when they knew the truth and realized He was going to give life to Lazarus, what reason could have moved Thomas to say, as did Peter in the garden: *Let us also go, that we may die with him?*[24] What are you saying, Holy Apostle? The Lord is not going to die; what do you fear? For Christ is not going to reprove but to perform an act of mercy, and therefore they cannot do Him harm. The Jews themselves could have reassured you, for when He rebuked them for wanting to stone him: *Many good works have I shewed you from my Father; for which of those works do you stone me?* They replied: *For a good work we stone thee not; but for blasphemy.*[25] For if they say they do not wish to stone him for His good works, and now He is going to perform one as good as giving life to Lazarus, what is it you fear, or

23 John 11:8–9.
24 John 11:16.
25 John 10:32–33.

why? Would it not be better to say: Let us go to enjoy the fruits of gratitude for the good work our Master is going to perform; to see Him applauded and thanked for the benefit; to see their wonderment at the miracle? And not to say what appears to be as irrelevant as: *Eamus et nos, ut moriamur cum eo.* But oh! The saint feared as an intelligent man and spoke as an Apostle. Is Christ not going to perform a miracle? Well, what greater danger? It is less intolerable for pride to hear rebukes than for envy to see miracles. In everything I have said, illustrious señora, I do not wish to say (let no such foolishness find a place in me) that I have been persecuted for knowing, but only for loving knowledge and letters, because I have achieved neither.

At one time the Prince of the Apostles found himself so distant from wisdom it was indicated with an emphatic: *And Peter followed afar off*;[26] as far from the praise of the learned man as one known for his lack of intelligence: *Not knowing what he said*;[27] and even questioned regarding his knowledge of wisdom, he himself said he knew nothing of it: *Woman, I know him not. Man, I know not what thou sayest.*[28] And what happens to him? As a result of being known as an ignorant man, he did not have the good fortune of a wise man but only the afflictions. Why? No reason was given

---

26 Luke 22:54.
27 Luke 9:33.
28 Luke 22:57 and 60.

other than: *This man was also with him.*[29] He loved wisdom, carried it in his heart, followed after it, valued being a follower and lover of wisdom; and although he was so far off that he did not understand or reach it, it was enough to incur its torments. There was always a foreign soldier to cause him distress, a maidservant to trouble him. I confess I find myself very far from the boundaries of wisdom and have wanted to follow it, although at a distance. Yet this has brought me closer to the fire of persecution, the crucible of torment, to the extent that some have requested that I be forbidden to study.

This once was achieved by a very saintly, very ingenuous mother superior who believed that study was a matter for the Inquisition and ordered me to stop. I obeyed (for the three months her power to command lasted) in that I did not pick up a book, but not studying at all, which is not in my power, I could not do, because although I did not study books, I studied all the things God created, and these were my letters, and my book was the entire mechanism of the universe. I saw nothing without reflecting on it, heard nothing without considering it, even the smallest material things, for there is no creature, no matter how low, in which one does not recognize *God created me*, none that does not astonish the understanding, if one considers it as one should. And so, I repeat, I looked at and admired

29 Luke 22:56.

everything; as a consequence, even the people to whom I spoke, and the things they said to me, gave rise to a thousand considerations: What is the origin of the varieties of intelligence and wit, since we are all one species? What could be the temperaments and hidden qualities that caused them? If I saw a figure, I would combine the proportion of its lines and measure it with my understanding and reduce it to other, different figures. I would walk sometimes in the front part of our dormitory (which is a very spacious room) and observe that while the lines of its two sides were parallel and the ceiling level, the eye made it seem that its lines inclined toward each other and the ceiling was lower at a distance than nearby, and from this I inferred that visual lines run straight, not parallel, but form a pyramidal shape instead. And I wondered whether this might be the reason the ancients were obliged to doubt the world was round. Because although it seems so, our sight could deceive us, showing concavities where there might not be any.

I notice everything in this manner and always have and have no control over it; in fact it tends to annoy me, for it wearies my head; I thought this, and composing verses, happened to everyone, until experience showed me the contrary; and this is so much my character or custom that I see nothing without considering it further. Two little girls were playing with a top in my presence, and no sooner did I see the movement and shape than I began, with this madness of mine, to consider the easy motion of the spherical shape and how the already transmitted impulse could last, independent of its cause, for far from the hand of the little girl, which was the motivating cause, the top still danced; not content with this, I had some flour brought in and sifted, so that as the top danced on top of it, I could learn whether the circles described by its movement were perfect or not; and I found that they were merely spiral lines that lost their circular nature as the impulse diminished. Some other girls were playing jackstraws (which is the most frivolous of children's games); I began to contemplate the figures they formed, and seeing that by chance three fell into a triangle, I began to connect one to the other, recalling that some say this was the shape of the mysterious ring of Solomon, which had distant indications and representations of the Holy Trinity, allowing him to perform countless miracles and marvels; and it is said that the harp of David had the same shape, and for that reason Saul was healed at its sound; harps in our day still have almost the same shape.

And what could I tell you, señora, about the natural secrets I have discovered when cooking? Seeing that an egg sets and fries in butter or oil but falls apart in syrup; seeing that for sugar to remain liquid it is enough to add a very small amount of water in which a quince or other bitter fruit has been placed; seeing that the yolk and the white of the same egg are so different that each can be mixed with sugar but together they cannot. I do not mean to tire you with these inconsequentialities, which I mention only to give you a complete view of my nature, and which I believe will cause you to laugh; but, señora, what can we women know but kitchen philosophies? As Lupercio Leonardo[30] so wisely said, one can philosophize very well and prepare supper. And seeing these minor details, I say that if Aristotle had cooked, he would have written a great deal more. Returning to my continual cogitation, I repeat that this is so constant in me I do not need books; on one occasion, because of a serious stomach ailment, the doctors prohibited my studying; after a few days I suggested to them that it would be less harmful to allow me books, because my cogitations were so strong and vehement that they consumed more energy in a quarter of an hour than studying books did in four days; and so they were persuaded to allow me to read. And further, señora: not even my sleep was free of this continual movement of my imaginative faculty; rather, it tends to operate more freely and unencumbered, examining with greater clarity and tranquility the images of the day, arguing, and composing verses, and I could offer you a large catalogue of them and the arguments and delicate points I have formulated more successfully asleep than awake, but I put those aside in order not to weary you, for what I have said is enough for your intelligence and per-

30 The citation should be attributed to Luperico's brother Bartolomé Leonardo de Argensola, Satire I.

spicacity to penetrate and see perfectly my entire nature, as well as the origin, means, and state of my studies.

If these, señora, are merits (I see them celebrated as such in men), they would not be so in me, because I act out of necessity. If they are blameworthy, for the same reason I believe I am not at fault; nonetheless, I am so wary of myself that in this or anything else I do not trust my own judgment; and so I remit the decision to your sovereign talent, submitting to whatever sentence you may impose, without contradiction or opposition, for this has been no more than a simple narrative of my inclination toward letters.

III

I confess as well that since this is so true, as I have said, I needed no examples, yet the many I have read, in both divine and human letters, have not failed to help me. For I find Deborah issuing laws, both military and political, and governing a people that had many learned men. I find an exceedingly wise Queen of Sheba, so learned she dares to test with enigmas the wisdom of the greatest of wise men and is not rebuked for that reason; instead, because of it, she becomes judge of the unbelievers. I find numerous illustrious women: some adorned with the gift of prophecy, like Abigail; others, with the gift of persuasion, like Esther; others, with piety, like Rahab; others, with perseverance, like Hannah, mother of Samuel, and countless others possessing all kinds of gifts and virtues.

If I turn to the Gentiles, I first encounter the Sibyls, chosen by God to prophesy the principal mysteries of our faith, in verses so learned and elegant they enthrall our admiration. I find a woman like Minerva, daughter of the foremost god Jupiter and mistress of all the knowledge of Athens, worshipped as goddess of the sciences. I find Polla Argentaria, who helped Lucan, her husband, write the great Pharsalia. I find the daughter of the divine Tiresias, more learned than her father. I find Zenobia, queen of the Palmyrenes, as wise as she was valiant. Arete, the most learned daughter of Aristippus. Nicostrata, inventor of Latin characters and extremely erudite in Greek ones. Aspasia of Miletus, who taught philosophy and rhetoric and was the tutor of the philosopher Pericles. Hypatia, who taught astronomy and studied for many years in Alexandria. Leontion, a Greek woman who wrote arguments countering the philosopher Theophrastus, which convinced him. Jucia,[31] Corinna, Cornelia, in short, all the great number of women who deserved fame, whether as Greeks, muses, or pythonesses, for all of them were simply learned women, considered and celebrated and also venerated as such in antiquity. Not to mention countless others who fill the books, for I find the Egyptian Catherine studying and affecting all the

31 Sor Juana may have meant Julia (Domna), an intellectual Roman empress.

wisdom of the wise men of Egypt. I find Gertrude reading, writing, and teaching. And for examples closer to home, I find a most holy mother of mine, Paula, learned in the Hebrew, Greek, and Latin languages and extremely skilled in interpreting Scripture. And none other than the great Saint Jerome scarcely thought himself worthy of being her chronicler, for with the lively thought and energetic exactitude he brings to his explanations, he says: If all the members of my body were tongues, they would not suffice to publish the wisdom and virtue of Paula. The widow Blaesilla deserved the same praise, as did the illustrious virgin Eustochium, both daughters of this saint; the second, for her knowledge, was called Prodigy of the World. Fabiola, a Roman woman, was also extremely learned in Holy Scripture. Proba Faltonia, another Roman, wrote an elegant book, a cento of selections from Virgil, on the mysteries of our Holy Faith. It is well known that our queen, Doña Isabel, the wife of Alfonso X,[32] wrote on astronomy. And many others whom I omit in order not to cite what others have said (a vice I have always despised), for in our day the great Christina Alexandra, Queen of Sweden, as learned as she is valiant and magnanimous, and the Most Honorable Ladies the Duchess of Aveiro and the Countess of Villaumbrosa are all flourishing.

---

32 The wife of Alfonso X was Violante of Aragon, who did collaborate on Alfonso's astronomical treatises. Doña Isabel was the wife and queen of Ferdinand V.

The illustrious Doctor Arce (a professor of Scripture, eminent for his virtue and learning), in his *Studioso Bibliorum*, raises this question: Is it legitimate for women to dedicate themselves to the study of Holy Scripture and its interpretation? And he offers many judgments of saints that argue against this, in particular the statement of the Apostle: Let your women keep silence in the churches: for it is not permitted unto them to speak,[33] et cetera. Then he offers other judgments, including one by the same Apostle in Titus: *The aged women likewise, that they be in behavior as becometh holiness . . . teachers of good things,*[34] with interpretations of the holy fathers; and finally he prudently resolves that giving public lectures from a professor's chair and preaching from a pulpit are not legitimate for women, but that studying, writing, and teaching privately not only are legitimate but very advantageous and useful; it is obvious that this does not apply to all women but only to those whom God has favored with special virtue and prudence, who are mature and erudite and have the necessary talent and requisites for so sacred an occupation. And this is true not only for women, who are considered to be so incompetent, but for men as well, who for the simple fact of being men think they are wise: the interpretation of Scripture should be forbidden unless the men are very learned and

33 1 Corinthians 14:34.
34 Titus 2:3.

virtuous, with tractable, well-inclined natures; I believe that doing otherwise has resulted in countless sectarians and has been at the root of countless heresies, for there are many who study but remain ignorant, especially those whose natures are arrogant, restless, proud, and inclined toward innovations in religion (which turns away from innovations); and so, in order to say what no one else has said, they are not content until they utter a heresy. About them the Holy Spirit declares: *For wisdom will not enter into a malicious soul.*[35] Knowledge does these men more harm than ignorance would. A wise man said that the man who does not know Latin is not a complete fool, but the one who does is qualified to be one. And I would like to add that a fool becomes perfect (if foolishness can reach perfection) by studying his bit of philosophy and theology and having some idea of languages, making him a fool in many sciences and many languages, because a great fool cannot be contained in his mother tongue alone.

These men, I repeat, are harmed by studying because it places a sword in the hands of a madman; being a noble instrument for defense, in his hands it means his death and the death of many others. This is what divine letters became in the hands of the wicked Pelagius and the perverse Arius, the wicked Luther, and the other heresiarchs like our Doctor (he was never ours and never a doctor) Cazalla, all of them

35 Wisdom 1:4 (D-R).

harmed by knowledge because, although it is the best nourishment and life of the soul, just as the better the food in an unbalanced, overheated stomach, the more arid, fermented, and perverse the humors it creates, so it is with these evil men, for the more they study the worse the opinions they engender; their understanding is blocked by the very thing that should have nourished them, for they study a great deal and digest very little, not taking into account the limited vessel of their understanding. Regarding this the Apostle says: *For I say, by the grace that is given me, to all that are among you, not to be more wise than it behoveth to be wise, but to be wise unto sobriety, and according as God hath divided to everyone the measure of faith.*[36] And the truth is that the Apostle did not say this to women but to men; the *taceant*[37] is not only for women but for all those who are not very capable. My wanting to know as much as or more than Aristotle or Saint Augustine, if I do not have the aptitude of Saint Augustine or Aristotle, means that even if I study more than both of them, I not only will not succeed in my ambition, but the lack of proportion in my purpose will weaken and confuse the operation of my weak understanding.

Oh, if all of us—and I before anyone, for I am an ignorant woman—would take the measure of our talent before studying and (what is worse) writing with a voracious

---

36 Romans 12:3 (D-R).
37 Keep silence (see page 189, n. 34).

desire to equal and even surpass others, how little ambition would we have left and how many errors would we avoid and how many twisted intelligences would we not have in the world! And I place mine in first place, for if I knew as much as I should, I would not be writing this. And I insist I am doing so only to obey you, with so much misgiving that you owe me more for taking up my pen, having this fear, than you would if I had sent you more perfect works. It is good that this will be corrected by you; erase it, tear it up, and reprimand me, for I will value that more than all the vain applause others may offer me: *That just men shall correct me in mercy, and shall reprove me; but let not the oil of the sinner fatten my head.*[38]

And returning to our Arce, I say that he offers as confirmation of his opinion the words of my father Saint Jerome (*To Leta, Upon the Education of her Daughter*) where he says: Accustom her tongue while she is still young to the sweetness of the Psalms. Even the names through which she gradually will become accustomed to form her phrases should not be chosen by chance but selected and repeated with care; the prophets must be included, of course, and the Apostles as well, and all the Patriarchs beginning with Adam down to Matthew and Luke, so that as she practices other things she will be readying her memory for the future. Let your daily task be taken from the flower of the Scriptures. If the

38 Psalm 140:5 (D-R).

saint wanted a little girl who had barely begun to speak to be educated in this way, what would he want in his nuns and spiritual daughters? It is known very well in the above mentioned Eustochium and Fabiola and in Marcella, her sister Pacatula, and others whom the saint honors in his letters, exhorting them to this sacred exercise, as it is known in the cited letter where I noted that *reddat tibi pensum,* which affirms and agrees with the *bene docentes* of Saint Paul, for the *reddat tibi* of my great father makes it plain that the teacher of the little girl is to be Leta, her mother.

Oh, how much harm could be averted in our republic if older women were as learned as Leta and knew how to teach as Saint Paul and my father Saint Jerome advise! Since they do not, and given the extreme idleness in which our unfortunate women are left, if some parents wish to give their daughters more instruction than usual, necessity and the lack of learned older women obliges them to have male tutors teach their daughters how to read, write, count, play an instrument, and other skills, which results in a good amount of harm, as we see every day in lamentable examples of mismatched unions, for over time, with close dealings and communication, what was thought impossible tends to become conceivable. For this reason many parents choose to leave their daughters unlettered and uneducated rather than expose them to so notable a danger as familiarity with men, which could be avoided if there were learned older women, as Saint Paul desires, and instruction would be handed down from one female to another as occurs in the teaching of needlework and other customary skills.

For what disadvantage can there be in having an older woman learned in letters, whose conversation and customs are holy, directing the education of young girls? The alternative is allowing them to be lost through lack of instruction, or wishing to teach them by means as dangerous as male tutors, even when there is no more risk than the indecency of having a shy girl (who still blushes when her own father looks in her face) sit beside a strange man who will treat her with domestic familiarity and authoritative informality; the modesty required in dealings with men and their conversation is enough reason not to permit this kind of arrangement. I do not find that this form of instruction, when men teach women, can be without danger except in the severe tribunal of a confessional or the decent distance of pulpits or the remote learning from books, but not in immediate proximity. Everyone knows this is true; even so, it is allowed only because of the lack of educated older women; therefore, not having them does great harm. This should be considered by those who, attached to *Mulieres in Ecclesia taceant*, curse the women who learn and teach blasphemy, as if the Apostle himself had not said: *bene docentes*. Moreover, the prohibition came at a time when, as Eusebius indicates, in the early Church women would teach one another doctrine in the temples, and this sound caused some confusion when the Apostles preached; that is why they were ordered to be silent, as occurs now, when one does not pray aloud while the preacher delivers his sermon.

There is no doubt that to understand many passages of divine letters, one needs to know a good deal about the history, customs, ceremonies, proverbs, and even modes of speech of the times when they were written in order to comprehend the references and allusions of certain locutions. *Rend your heart, and not your garments,*[39] is this not an allusion to the ceremony the Hebrews had of tearing their clothes as a sign of grief, as the evil high priest did when he said that Christ had blasphemed?[40] In many passages the Apostle writes of help for widows, and did they also not refer to the customs of those times? The passage about the strong woman: *Her husband is known in the gates, when he sitteth among the elders of the land,*[41] does it not allude to the custom of holding the tribunal of judges at the gates of the cities? And *give your land to God*, did it not signify making a vow? *Hiemantes*, was this not the name given to public sinners, because they performed their penance in the open air, unlike others who repented in a covered passage? The complaint of Christ to the Pharisee regarding the lack of a kiss and the washing of his feet, was it not based on the custom the Jews had of doing these things? And countless

39 Joel 2:13.
40 Matthew 26:65: *Then the high priest rent his clothes, saying, He hath spoken blasphemy.*
41 Proverbs 31:23.

other passages that one encounters constantly, not only in divine letters but in human letters as well, such as *venerate the purple*, which meant obeying the king; *manumittere eum*, which means to emancipate, alluding to the custom and ceremony of slapping the slave to give him his freedom. And *intonuit coelum*,[42] in Virgil, alluding to the omen of thunder in the west, which was taken as a good sign. And *you never ate hare*,[43] in Martial, which has not only the charm of ambiguity in *leporem* but the allusion to the property the hare was said to possess. The proverb *Sailing the coast of Malia means forgetting what you have at home*, which alludes to the great danger of the promontory of Laconia. The reply of the chaste matron to the insistent suitor, *the hinges will not be greased on my account, nor will the torches be lit*, meaning she did not wish to marry, alluding to the ceremony of greasing doors with fat and lighting nuptial torches at weddings; as if we were to say today: no dowry will be paid on my account and the priest will give no blessings. There are so many comments of this kind in Virgil and Homer and all the poets and orators. And aside from this, what difficulties are not found in sacred passages, even in matters of grammar, such as using the plural for the singular, or moving from the second to the third person, as in the Song of Songs: *Let him kiss me with the kiss of his mouth, for thy breasts are better*

42 It has been suggested that this is a misprint for *intonuit laevum*, it thundered on the left.
43 It was believed that eating hare heightened a woman's beauty.

than wine?[44] Or placing adjectives in the genitive instead of the accusative, as in *I will take the chalice of salvation?*[45] Or using the feminine for the masculine, and calling any sin adultery?

All of this demands more instruction than some think who, as simple grammarians or at most with a few terms of formal logic, attempt to interpret Scriptures and seize on *Mulieres in Ecclesiis taceant*, not knowing how it is to be understood. Or *Let the woman learn in silence*,[46] this being a passage more in favor of women than against them, for it commands that they learn, and while they are learning, it is evident they must be silent. And it is also written: *Take heed and hearken, O Israel*,[47] where all men and women are addressed, and all are ordered to be silent, because the person who hears and learns of necessity must also attend and be silent. If this is not so, I should like these interpreters and expounders of Saint Paul to explain to me how they understand the passage *Mulieres in Ecclesia taceant*. Because they must understand it either as physical, the pulpits and cathedras,[48] or formal, the universality of the faithful, which is the Church. If they understand it in the first sense (which is, in my opinion, its true meaning, for we see that, in fact,

44 Song of Songs 1:1 (D-R).
45 Psalm 115:13.
46 1 Timothy 2:11.
47 Deuteronomy 27:9.
48 Bishops' official thrones.

women are not permitted to read publicly or preach in the Church), why reproach women who study privately? And if they understand it in the second and want the prohibition of the Apostle to be transcendent, so that not even in secret would women be permitted to write or study, why do we find that the Church has permitted Gertrude, Teresa, Birgitta, the Nun of Ágreda, and many other women to write? And if they tell me these women were saints, it is true, but that does not negate my argument; first, because the proposition of Saint Paul is absolute and embraces all women without excepting saints, for in his day there were also Martha and Mary, Marcella, Mary the mother of Jacob, Salome, and many others in the fervor of the early Church, and he does not exempt them; and now we find that the Church permits women who are saints and those who are not saints to write, for the Nun of Ágreda and Sor María de la Antigua are not canonized, and their writings circulate; neither were Saint Teresa and the others when they wrote, which means that the prohibition of Saint Paul was directed only at the public pulpits, for if the Apostle had prohibited writing, the Church would not have permitted it. Now, I do not have the courage to teach—for that would be excessive presumption in me—and writing requires greater talent than mine, and very great deliberation. As Saint Cyprian says: *The things we write demand the most careful consideration*. All that I have wished is to study in order to be ignorant about less: for, according to Saint Augustine, one learns some things in order to do them and others only to know them: *Discimus quaedam, ut sciamus; quaedam, ut faciamus.* Then where is my offense if I refrain even from what it is legitimate for women to do, which is to teach by writing, because I know I do not have the disposition to do so, following the advice of Quintilian: Let each person learn not only from the precepts of others but from his own nature?

If my crime lies in the *Athenagoric Letter*, did that do more than simply refer to my opinion with all the reverence I owe to our Holy Mother Church? If she, with her most holy authority, does not forbid me to do so, why should others? Expressing an opinion contrary to that of Vieira was insolence in me, and expressing an opinion contrary to that of three Holy Fathers of the Church was not insolence in his paternity? Is not my understanding, such as it is, as free as his, for it comes from the same soil? Is his opinion one of the revealed principles of our Holy Faith, so that we must believe it blindly? Moreover, I did not fail in the deference owed to so great a man, which his defender lacked in addressing me, having forgotten the judgment of Titus Lucius: Respect is companion to the arts;[49] nor did I criticize in any way the Sacred Company of Jesus; and I wrote only for the judgment of the one who suggested I do so; according to Pliny, the state of the person who publishes is not the same as that of one who merely speaks. For if I had thought the letter

---

49 Perhaps a misquotation of Quintillian's *Institutio Oratoria.*

would be published, it would not have been as carelessly written as it was. If it is, as the censor[50] says, heretical, why does he not denounce it? Then he would be avenged and I content, for I value more, as I should, the name of Catholic and obedient daughter of my Holy Mother Church than all the praise for being learned. If it is brutish—and they do well to say so—then let him laugh, even if it be with feigned laughter, for I do not tell him to praise me, and just as I was free to disagree with the opinion of Vieira, anyone else is free to disagree with mine.

But where is this taking me, señora? This does not apply here, and it is not for your ears, but since I am speaking of my accusers, I recalled the phrases of one, which appeared recently, and without being aware of it my pen slipped into an attempt to respond to him in particular, when my intent was to speak in general. And so, returning to our Arce, he says he learned of two nuns in this city: one in the Convent de Regina, who had memorized the breviary so well that she applied its verses, psalms, and the aphorisms and homilies of the saints with great quickness of mind and correctness in her conversation. The other, in the Convent de la Concepción, was so accustomed to reading the epistles of my father Saint Jerome, as well as the saint's words, that Arce says: I thought I heard Jerome himself, speaking in Spanish.

50 The identity of the "censor" is unknown, though some speculate it may be the Bishop of Puebla ("Sor Filotea") himself.

And about her he says that he learned, after her death, that she had translated the epistles into Spanish; and it pains him that talents like these had not been used in greater studies with philosophical principles, and he does not say the name of either one, although he alludes to them as confirmation of his judgment, which is that not only is it legitimate but very useful and necessary for women to study sacred letters, nuns in particular, which is what you in your wisdom exhort me to do, and with which so many authorities concur.

If I turn to my ability, so often criticized, to make verses—which is so natural in me that I even have to force myself not to write this letter in verse, and I might say: Everything I wished to say took the form of verse[51]—seeing it condemned and incriminated so often by so many, I have searched very diligently for what may be the harm in it and have not found it; rather, I find verses in the mouths of the Sybils applauded, and sanctified in the pens of the prophets, especially King David, about whom the great expositor and my beloved father says, explaining the measure of his meters: In the manner of Horace and Pindar, now it races in iambs, now the alcaic resounds, now it rises in sapphic, now it moves forward with broken feet.[52] Most of the sacred books are in meter, such as the Books of Moses, and Saint Isidore says, in his *Etymologiae*, that the Book of Job is in

51 Ovid.
52 St. Jerome, preface to *Chronicle* (written c. 380 CE).

heroic verse. Solomon wrote the *Song of Songs* in verse, as did Jeremiah the *Lamentations*. For this reason, says Cassiodorus: All poetic locutions originate in Holy Scripture. Our Catholic Church not only does not scorn verses but uses them in its hymns and recites those of Saint Ambrose, Saint Thomas, Saint Isidore, and others. Saint Bonaventure was so fond of them that there is scarcely a page of his that does not contain verses. It is evident that Saint Paul studied them, for he cites and translates verses of Aratus: *For in him we live, and move, and have our being,*[53] and cites another by Parmenides: *The Cretans are always liars, evil beasts, slow bellies.*[54] Saint Gregory Nazianzen argues questions of matrimony and virginity in elegant verses. Why should I grow weary? The Queen of Wisdom and Our Lady, with her sacred lips, intoned the Canticle of the Magnificat; and having presented her as an example, it would be an offense to present profane examples, although they may be very serious and learned men, for this is more than enough proof; and seeing that, although Hebrew elegance could not fit into Latin measure, for which reason the holy translator, more attentive to the importance of the meaning, omitted the verse, but even so, the psalms retain the name and divisions of verses; then where is the harm in them? Because the art is not to blame for its evil use but the one who professes

53 Acts 17:28.
54 Titus 1:12.

evil and debases it, making it a snare of the devil; and this occurs in all the arts and sciences.

If the evil lies in a woman writing verses, it is clear that many have done so in a praiseworthy way; where is the evil in my being a woman? Of course I confess that I am base and despicable, but in my judgment no verse of mine has been called indecent. Moreover, I have never written anything of my own free will but only because others have entreated and ordered me to; I do not recall having written for my own pleasure except for a trifle they called *The Dream*. The letter that you, my lady, so honored was written with more repugnance than anything else, because it dealt with sacred matters for which (as I have said) I have a reverent awe, and because it seemed to impugn, something for which I feel a natural aversion. And I believe that if I could have foreseen the fortunate destiny to which it was born—for, like another Moses, I abandoned it in the waters of the Nile of silence, where it was found and treated lovingly by a princess like you—I believe, I repeat, that if I had thought this would happen, I would have drowned it first with the same hands from which it was born, for fear the awkward blunders of my ignorance would be seen in the light of your wisdom. In this the greatness of your kindness is revealed, for your will applauds precisely what your brilliant understanding must reject. But now that its fate has brought it to your door, so abandoned and orphaned that you even had to give it a name, I regret that along with my imperfections, it also bears the defects of haste, not only because of my continuing ill health and the countless duties my obedience imposes, and because I lack someone to help me write and feel the need for everything to be in my own hand, and because writing it went against my nature and all I wanted was to keep my promise to one I could not disobey, I did not have the time to refine it; as a consequence I failed to include entire discourses and many proofs that I had at hand but did not add in order to stop writing; and if I had known it would be printed, I would not have omitted them, if only in order to satisfy certain objections that have been raised, which I could dispatch, but I shall not be so discourteous as to place such indecent objects before the purity of your eyes, for it is enough that I offend them with my ignorance without adding the insolence of others. If they happen to fly to you (for they are so light in weight they may), then I shall do as you command; for if it does not contravene your precepts, I shall never take up the pen in my own defense, because it seems to me that one offense does not require another in response, when one recognizes error in the very place it lies hidden, for as my father Saint Jerome says, Good discourse does not seek secrets,[55] and Saint Ambrose: Concealment is in the nature of a guilty conscience. Nor do I consider myself refuted, for a precept of the Law says: An accusation does not endure if not tended by the person who made it. What

55 St. Jerome, letter to Pacatula (written 413 CE).

certainly is worth pondering is the effort it has required to make copies. A strange madness to put more effort into stripping away approval than acquiring it! I, señora, have not wanted to respond, although others have without my knowledge: it is enough that I have seen some papers, among them one that I send to you because it is learned and because reading it makes up in part for the time you have wasted on what I write. If you, señora, would like me to do the opposite of what I have put forward for your judgment and opinion, at the slightest sign of what you desire my intention will cede, as it ought to; it was, as I have said, to be silent, for although Saint John Chrysostom says: Slanderers must be refuted, and those who question taught, I see that Saint Gregory also says: It is no less a victory to tolerate enemies than to overcome them; and that patience conquers by tolerating and triumphs by suffering. And if among the Roman Gentiles it was the custom, at the height of the glory of its captains—when they entered in triumph over other nations, dressed in purple and crowned with laurel, their carriages pulled not by animals but by crowned, conquered kings, accompanied by spoils of the riches of the entire world, and the conquering army adorned with the insignias of its feats, hearing the applause of the people in their honorary titles of renown, such as Fathers of the Nation, Columns of Empire, Walls of Rome, Protectors of the Republic, and other glorious names—for a soldier, in this supreme moment of human glory and happiness, to say aloud to the conqueror, with his consent and by order of the Senate: "Remember that you are mortal; remember that you have these defects," not forgetting the most shameful, which is what occurred in the triumph of Caesar, when the lowest soldiers called out in his hearing: "Beware, Romans, we bring you the bald adulterer." This was done so that in the midst of countless honors the conqueror would not become vain, the ballast of these insults would counterbalance the sails of so much praise, and the ship of good judgment would not founder in the winds of acclaim. And I say that if Gentiles did this with only the light of natural law, we who are Catholics, with the precept of loving our enemies, what would we not do to tolerate them? For my part I can assure you that at times calumny has mortified me but never done me harm, because I take for a great fool the person who, having the opportunity to gain merit, endures the great effort and loses the merit, which is like those who do not wish to accept death and in the end die; their resistance does nothing to exempt them from death, but it does take away the merit of resignation and turns what might have been a good death into one that was bad. And so, señora, I believe these things do more good than harm, and consider the effect of praise on human weakness a greater risk, for it tends to appropriate what is not ours, and we need to take great care to keep the words of the Apostle etched in our hearts: *And what hast thou that thou didst not receive? Now if thou didst receive it, why dost thou glory, as if thou hadst not received it?*[56] so they can serve as a shield that resists the sharp points of praise, which are like lances that, when not attributed to God, to Whom they belong, take our life and turn us into thieves of the honor of God and usurpers of the talents He gave us and the gifts He lent us, for which we must give a strict accounting. And so, señora, I fear praise more than calumny, because calumny, with only a simple act of patience, is transformed into benefit, while praise requires many acts of reflection and humility and knowledge of oneself to keep it from doing harm. In my case, I know and recognize that knowing this is a special favor of God, allowing me to behave in both instances according to the judgment of Saint Augustine: One should not believe the friend who praises or the enemy who censures.[57] Although most of the time, given my nature, I squander what I have been given or combine it with so many defects and imperfections that I debase the good that came from Him. And so, in the little of mine that has been printed, not only my name but consent for the printing has been not of my own choosing but the will of another who does not fall under my control, as in the printing of the *Athenagoric Letter*; this means that only some *Exercises of the Incarnation* and *Offerings of the Sorrows* were printed for public devotion with my approval, but without my name; I

56 1 Corinthians 4:7.
57 St. Augustine, Answer to the Letters of Petilian the Dentist (written c. 400 CE).

am sending copies of these to you, to give (if you agree) to our sisters the nuns of your holy community and others in the city. I am sending only one copy of the *Sorrows* because the others have been distributed and I could find no other. I wrote them years ago, solely for the devotions of my sisters, and afterward they became more widely known; their subjects are so much greater than my mediocrity and ignorance, and the only thing that helped me with them was that they dealt with our great Queen: it is notable that the iciest heart is set ablaze when one alludes to Most Holy Mary. I should like, illustrious señora, to send you works worthy of your virtue and wisdom, but as the poet said:

> *Although strength may be lacking, the will must be praised.*
> *I think the gods are satisfied with that.*[58]

If I write any other trifles, they will always seek out the sanctuary of your feet and the security of your correction, for I have no other jewel with which to pay you, and as Seneca says, whoever begins to offer benefits is obliged to continue them; in this way, your own generosity will repay you, for only in this way can I be freed in an honorable manner from my debt and avoid this warning from the same Seneca: It is shameful to be surpassed in benefits.[59] For it is the magna-

58 Ovid.
59 Seneca, *De Beneficiis*, V:2.

nimity of the generous creditor to give the poor debtor what is needed to satisfy the debt. This is what God gave to the world incapable of repaying Him: He gave his own Son so that He would receive a recompense worthy of Him.

If the style of this letter, illustrious señora, has not been what you deserve, I beg your pardon if in the homely familiarity or lack of respect in my treating you as a veiled nun, one of my sisters, I have forgotten the distance of your most eminent person, for if I had seen you without the veil, this would not have happened; but you, with your wisdom and kindness, will supply or amend the words, and if *vos*[60] seems incongruous, I used it because it seemed that for the reverence I owe you, *Your Reverence* shows very little reverence; change it then to whatever seems honorable and what you deserve, for I have not dared to exceed the limits of your style or go past the boundary of your modesty.

Keep me in your grace and pray for divine grace for me and may the Lord grant you a large portion of it and keep you, which is my plea and my need. From this convent of our father Saint Jerome in Mexico City, on the first day of the month of March in the year 1691. I kiss your hand and am your most favored

Juana Inés de la Cruz

60 Sor Juana uses the familiar form of the second person singular, *vos*, reserved for informal and familiar relations.

PERSONS, PLACES, AND
PERSONIFICATIONS

*The page number at the end of each entry gives the first reference in
this translation.*

AULUS GELLIUS (c. 125–180 CE), Roman author and grammarian, 178

AVEIRO, DUCHESS OF (1630–1715), Strong-minded noblewoman who resisted efforts to deny her control of the House of Aveiro and its estates, 188

BELLONA, Roman goddess of war, 16

BIRGITTA, SAINT (1303–1373), Mystic and the founder of the Bridgettine nuns and monks, 198

BLAESILLA (d. 384 CE), Daughter of St. Paula of Rome, a follower of St. Jerome, 188

BOETHIUS (c. 480–524 CE), Roman philosopher, 147

BONAVENTURE, SAINT (c. 1218–1274), Italian theologian canonized in 1482 and declared a Doctor of the Church in 1588, 202

CAMPASPE, Mistress of Alexander the Great, 148

CASSIODORUS (c. 490–c. 585 CE), Roman official and monk, 202

CATHERINE, SAINT (fl. 4th century CE), Catherine of Alexandria; scholar and virgin saint, 187

CATO, Cato the Younger (95–46 BCE); Roman official famous for his moral integrity, 17

CAZALLA, DR. AGUSTÍN (1510–1559), Spanish Lutheran, 190

CERDA (1221–1284), Noble family that traces its origin to Fernando, son of Alfonso X, King of Castile and Leon, 16

CÉSAR MENESES (first name Sebastião, d. 1671), Archbishop of Lisbon, 143

CHRISTINA ALEXANDRA (1626–1689), Queen of Sweden with an interest in books and science, 188

CICERO (106–43 BCE), Roman politician, philosopher, and orator, 51

CONSTANTINE (c. 272–337 CE), Constantine the Great; first Roman emperor to convert to Christianity; founder of the Byzantine Empire, 15

CORINNA (fl. 5th century BCE), Ancient Greek poet, thought by some to be a contemporary of Pindar, 187

CORNELIA, Early Catholic saint and martyr, 187

CYPRIAN, SAINT (c. 200–258 CE), Bishop of Carthage, 198

DEBORAH, Female judge of ancient Israel, named in Judges 4–5, 186

ESTHER, Jewish queen of Persia (wife of Ahasuerus) who risked her life to save Jewish citizens from slaughter by the vizier Haman, as described in the Book of Esther, 186

EUSEBIUS (OF CAESAREA) (c. 260–c. 339 CE), Palestinian scholar and
historian of the early Church, 194

EUSTOCHIUM (c. 368–420 CE), Daughter of St. Paula, a saint, and a
Desert Mother, 188

FABIOLA (d. 399 CE), Roman noblewoman who became a follower of
St. Jerome and St. Paula, 188

GALEN (129–c. 199 CE), Most famous physician of antiquity, 95

GALVE, COUNTESS OF, Vicerine of New Spain (Mexico); her husband
reigned 1688–1696, 20

GERSON, Jean Charlier (1363–1429), French theologian, 146

GERTRUDE, St. Gertrude of Helfta (1256–1302); German mystic and
theologian, 188

GÓNGORA, Luis de Góngora y Argote (1561–1627); influential Spanish
poet, 77

GRACIÁN, Baltasar Gracián y Morales (1601–1658); Spanish writer and
philosopher, 177

GREGORY, SAINT, known as St. Gregory the Great (540–640 CE);
pope from 590 to 604, 205

GREGORY OF NAZIANZUS, SAINT, Gregory Nanzianzen (540–604 CE);
Doctor of the Church, he was Archbishop of Constantinople, 144

HANNAH, Woman who conceived her son miraculously at an advanced
age, as described in 1 Samuel 1, 187

HARPOCRATES, Egyptian god of silence and, by extension, night,
depicted with his finger to his lips, 80

HELENA, Empress (c. 248–c. 328 CE), mother of Constantine, and
saint, 15

HYPATIA (c. 370–415 CE), Neoplatonist and mathematician in Roman
Egypt, 187

ICARUS, In Greek mythology, made himself wings of feathers and wax
but flew too close to the sun; the wax melted, and he fell into the
sea, 74

ISABEL, DOÑA, co-ruler, with King Ferdinand V, of Castile and Leon,
188

ISIDORE, SAINT (c. 560–636 CE), Archbishop of Seville who com-
posed the encyclopedic *Etymologiae* that collected numerous frag-
ments of classical knowledge, 201

(1515–1582); a prominent mystic and writer, she was canonized in 1622 and declared a Doctor of the Church in 1970, 144

THAIS, SAINT; 4th-century repentant courtesan who lived in Alexandria, Egypt, 34

THEMIS, Greek titaness, daughter of heaven and earth, 99

THEOPHRASTUS (c. 372–c. 287 BCE), Student of Aristotle in the Peripatetic school of philosophy, 187

TIRESIAS, In Greek mythology, a blind prophet who was transformed into a woman for seven years, 187

VIEIRA, FATHER ANTONIO DE (1608–1697), Well-known Portuguese preacher, 143

VILLAUMBROSA, COUNTESS OF, Helped to found a convent in 1670, 188

ZENOBIA (240–c. 275 CE), Queen of the Palmyrene Empire in Syria, she conquered Egypt and led a revolt against Rome, 187